CSR, Sustainability, Ethics & Governance

Series Editors

Samuel O. Idowu, London Metropolitan University, Calcutta House, London, UK

René Schmidpeter, BFH, Bern, Switzerland

In recent years the discussion concerning the relation between business and society has made immense strides. This has in turn led to a broad academic and practical discussion on innovative management concepts, such as Corporate Social Responsibility, Corporate Governance and Sustainability Management. This series offers a comprehensive overview of the latest theoretical and empirical research and provides sound concepts for sustainable business strategies. In order to do so, it combines the insights of leading researchers and thinkers in the fields of management theory and the social sciences and from all over the world, thus contributing to the interdisciplinary and intercultural discussion on the role of business in society. The underlying intention of this series is to help solve the world's most challenging problems by developing new management concepts that create value for business and society alike. In order to support those managers, researchers and students who are pursuing sustainable business approaches for our common future, the series offers them access to cutting-edge management approaches. CSR, Sustainability, Ethics and Governance is accepted by the Norwegian Register for Scientific Journals, Series and Publishers, maintained and operated by the Norwegian Social Science Data Services (NSD).

Haifeng Huang · Samuel O Idowu · Hao Sun ·
Chuanbing Zhou · Yang Li · Zhangchen Wang

Waste Management for Global Sustainability

A Comparative Analysis of China-US Policies and Practices

Springer

Haifeng Huang
Wilson Center
Washington, DC, USA

Hao Sun
School of Civic Leadership, Business, &
Social Change
Gallaudet University
Washington, DC, USA

Yang Li
Haas School of Business
University of California
Berkeley, CA, USA

Samuel O Idowu
Guildhall School of Business & Law
London Metropolitan University
London, UK

Chuanbing Zhou
Research Center for Eco-Environmental
Science
Chinese Academy of Sciences
Beijing, China

Zhangchen Wang
Institute for China-America Studies
Washington, DC, USA

ISSN 2196-7075 ISSN 2196-7083 (electronic)
CSR, Sustainability, Ethics & Governance
ISBN 978-981-96-8304-8 ISBN 978-981-96-8305-5 (eBook)
https://doi.org/10.1007/978-981-96-8305-5

This Springer imprint is published by the registered company Springer Nature Singapore Pte Ltd.
The registered company address is: 152 Beach Road, #21-01/04 Gateway East, Singapore 189721, Singapore

Our book is dedicated to:

- *Professor John B. Cobb, Jr. (1925–2024), renowned American ecologist and academician*
- *Professor Gernot Gutmann (1929–2024), German economist*
- *Professor Roland Felber (1935–2001), German historian*
- *Professor Baoxu Zhao (1922–2012), Chinese political scientist*
- *Professor Wentang Du (1935–2017), Chinese historian*

Their pioneering contributions to sustainable development theory have provided the intellectual foundation for this work.

Foreword

This book represents a pioneering contribution to the study of municipal solid waste and the policies that can mitigate its negative impact on both the environment and the economy. By drawing a comparative analysis between China and the United States—the two largest economies and the biggest contributors to greenhouse gas emissions—this research sheds light on an often overlooked but critically important area of environmental policy. The findings presented here offer a new and effective approach to addressing the environmental and social challenges posed by municipal waste, providing insights that are essential for meaningful and lasting change.

This research is structured around a comprehensive exploration of municipal waste in both countries. First, the authors analyze the trends and types of municipal waste in China and the U.S., focusing on the methods of disposal and the environmental and health threats posed by plastic and food waste. They then delve into the economic costs associated with these types of waste. Following this overview, the focus shifts to food waste, which is the largest source of greenhouse gas emissions within the municipal waste category. This section compares emission trends, calculation methods, and policies aimed at reducing food waste and its associated emissions. The book also includes case studies from businesses and non-governmental organizations (NGOs) that have implemented successful food waste mitigation strategies.

In the subsequent section, the authors turn to plastic waste, with particular attention paid to the policies in both China and the U.S. aimed at reducing single-use plastics. Finally, they offer a set of concrete policy recommendations that span regulatory frameworks, measurement systems, technological innovations, financing strategies, and market-based approaches. The book advocates a hybrid governance model that combines government regulation with market incentives, creating a dynamic system in which waste is not only managed but also converted into renewable energy, creating a win-win outcome that benefits both the economy and the environment.

Greenhouse gas emissions are widely acknowledged as a major contributor to global warming and worsening natural disasters. However, despite ambitious emission-reduction targets set by many policymakers, the emissions resulting from municipal waste have largely been neglected. This research addresses that gap by examining such emissions in the context of China and the U.S., two countries whose municipal waste management practices are critical to global environmental efforts. Additionally, the volume places significant emphasis on plastic waste, recognizing its crucial role in shaping comprehensive waste management strategies. By comparing the municipal waste management practices of the U.S. and China, this research provides valuable insights for policymakers seeking to develop practical and effective policies.

In this context, I first proposed the sustainable development triangle at the 1992 Rio Earth Summit, which integrates environmental, social, and economic perspectives into policy. I have also supported global efforts to address climate change, including contributions to the IPCC Climate Change Reports over 3 decades, and work with the World Bank and other governmental and non-governmental institutions. As a strong supporter of sustainable development and balanced inclusive green growth (BIGG), I particularly appreciate the book's focus on converting waste and emissions into renewable energy, which not only addresses environmental challenges but also facilitates the transition to sustainable energy systems. More broadly, I commend the authors for their thorough examination of municipal waste management. This often overlooked topic has tremendous potential to address a wide range of issues (including pollution, GHG emissions, recycling, health, energy supply, etc.), thereby contributing to all three aspects of sustainability—economic, social and environmental.

While this work makes a significant contribution to the field, it also helps identify gaps and areas for further research, including other types of municipal solid waste, various investment challenges, and technical difficulties involved in converting waste into renewable energy. In conclusion, I believe that this book will inspire new thinking among policymakers, researchers and the concerned public, while contributing to the collective efforts needed to promote global sustainable development and reduce the catastrophic effects of climate change.

Mohan Munasinghe
Chairman, Munasinghe Institute for Development (MIND) and MIND Group, Vice Chair, IPCC that shared the 2007 Nobel Peace prize, 2021 Blue Planet prize Laureate
Colombo, Sri Lanka

Preface

The old business model used by corporate entities for many centuries from the period of Industrial Revolution—1750–1830 until recently was based on a totally wrong and unsustainable assumption. It assumed that the planet Earth was able to generate and process its wastes sustainably without any environmental consequences or perhaps they were oblivious to those consequences. Many of the environmental challenges that ensued have proved this assumption to be wrong and unsustainable. With this wrong assumption, resources were taken, used and the wastes that emanated from them discarded carelessly with no thoughts for their future environmental impacts. For example, old cars, televisions, refrigerators, plastic bags and bottles etc. were dumped either on land or in the sea. What an unsustainable way to exist on this our precious planet?

It has been argued that the very high volume of the municipal waste we generate globally would increase from its present high level by 70% if no concerted actions were taken to sustainably deal with the waste. This study on ***A comparative Analysis of the policies and practices of Waste Management in the People's Republic of China and the United States of America*** is a great contribution to the global attempts of finding solutions to all the ensuing challenges we worry about in terms of waste management.

We are constantly reminded of the adverse impacts of global warming, climate change, pollution bio-diversity loss and many fatal and life threatening occurrences in the form of disasters that have ensued as a result of these problems in different parts of the world. It is imperative that more studies like this one are necessary in different parts of the globe. We need to know more about the problems and what nation states are doing in terms of their policies and practices.

It is hoped that the study on waste management in two of the largest economies in the world would provide a deep understanding of how these Chinese and Americans dealing with the global challenge of waste management.

August 2025

Haifeng Huang
Washington, USA

Samuel O Idowu
London, UK

Hao Sun
Washington, USA

Chuanbing Zhou
Beijing, USA

Yang Li
Berkeley, USA

Zhangchen Wang
Washington, USA

Acknowledgements

This report detailing the collaborative efforts between the Peoples' Republic of China and the United States of America in order to provide sustainable solutions to waste management challenges is the culmination of joint efforts and significant contributions from numerous individuals and organizations.

We wish to extend my deepest appreciation to the following individuals and groups:

- **The Woodrow Wilson International Center for Scholars**, Special thanks to Jennifer Turner, Director, the Wilson Center of China Environment Forum, and to Fellows of the Centre, Steven Jackson, and Karen Mancl for their invaluable guidance, support, and detailed feedback, which were instrumental throughout the research journey. We are deeply appreciative of the continued encouragement and support from the Center's leaders and colleagues, especially during the challenging times of the COVID-19 pandemic. Their unwavering support enabled a successful completion of the research project. We also wish to acknowledge the strong support received in terms of library materials and an excellent research environment from Robert Litwak, Senior Vice President, and Kent Hughes, former Director of the Program on America and the Global Economy. Additionally, our sincere thanks go to Kimberly Conner, Lindsay Collins, Beverly Thomas, Claudia Del Pozo, Maria-Stella Gatzoulis, Nancy Walker, Michelle Kamalich, Andrea Britten, and Jennifer Nguyen for their assistance and support.
- **The dedicated research teams from various universities across the US and China, including**, Xihao ZHAO, Jiayi ZHOU, Xiaoxiao ZHANG, Yunhuan CHEN, Wenqing LIN, Zirui LIU, Yuxin QU, Chad HIGGENBOTOTTOM, Kai MIRCHANDANI, Dong CHEN and Wei ZHANG. Their relentless research efforts and effective coordination with diverse stakeholders added depth and breadth to this report.
- **Esteemed research scholars**, such as Mohan MUNASINGHE (the 2021 Blue Planet Prize Laureate and Vice Chair of the UN Intergovernmental Panel on Climate Change), Gerhard STAHL (the former Secretary-General of the Committee of the regions of the European Union), Zhaochun JIANG (Research

Fellow of Chinese Academy of Sciences). Thanks for the strong support in topic selection, research methods or recommendations in the early stages of the research.

- **Chinese Research Partners**: Qiyong Xu (Professor of School of Environment and Energy at Peking University Shenzhen Graduate School) and Huanan Wu (Peking University), Haiying Lin (Hainan University), Hualiang Lu (Nanjing Audit University), Tao Hu (Director of Lakestone Institute for Sustainable Development) and Yalong Zhang (Director of Shenzhen Institute of Sustainable Development). Their engagement in insightful discussions and provision of access to pivotal resources and information were invaluable.
- **Various governmental and non-governmental organizations** that contributed their experiences, data, and case studies, thereby enriching this report with practical insights and compelling evidence. Contributions from individuals such as Feng Jia (former director and chief expert of the Publicity and Education Center of the Ministry of Ecology and Environment) , Gendong Shi (Executive Director of the UNESCO Secretariat for Education for Sustainable Development in China), Susan Fife-Ferris (Director of Solid Waste Planning & Program of Seattle Public Utilities), Fujin Zhou (Principal Economist of Solid Waste Performance & Analytics, City of Seattle), Xuehua Zhang, Laura Jackson (Lead Administrative Specialist of Maryland Environmental Service), Erin Simon (Vice President and Head of World Wildlife Fund), Mahmudul Hasan (Chief Technical Officer at the Baltimore City Department of Public Works), and Martha Ainsworth (Chair of the Maryland Sierra Club Zero Waste Team) were particularly noteworthy.

We are especially grateful to all the scientists, researchers, and policymakers who dedicated their time and expertise, transforming this report into a comprehensive tool for advancing US-China collaboration in waste management and environmental conservation.

Finally, we extend our gratitude to everyone who offered feedback and support, thereby shaping this report into a significant contribution to the realms of environmental policy and international cooperation. We are also grateful to our colleagues and friends at Springer Nature, Director of Books, Christian Rauscher, Dr Prashanth Mahagaonkar, Barbara Bethke and RocioTorregrosa for their continued support all these great projects of ours.

Corresponding author: Professor Hao Sun, Ph.D., Gallaudet University (hao.sun@gallaudet.edu)

Executive Summary

In the face of the ongoing "triple planetary crisis" of climate change, biodiversity loss, and rampant pollution, heightened consumerism and flawed waste management practices contribute significantly to worsening global environmental and health conditions. Waste management, a critical component of environmental conservation and sustainable development, is increasingly challenging, with burgeoning volumes of municipal solid waste (MSW) exacerbated by rapid urbanization and population growth. Notably, plastic and food waste, due to their abundance and environmental persistence, pose particularly acute issues. Within this context, the pivotal roles of the United States and China—two of the world's largest waste producers—provide a unique lens to explore effective management strategies, practices, and policies to mitigate these crises. This report conducts a comprehensive comparative analysis of waste management trends between the U.S. and China, assessing their approaches from municipal waste generation to policy frameworks, with a focus on collaboration for enhancing global waste management and sustainability.

Significant Findings and Collaborative Opportunities:

1. Urban Waste Management Trends

   Both the U.S. and China rank highest in global municipal solid waste generation, reflecting their extensive consumer culture and urban populations. While China reported approximately 212 million tons and the U.S. about 266 million tons of MSW in 2018, contrasting waste composition, management practices, and policy approaches underscore their divergent paths toward waste management efficiency and sustainability. This divergence offers a ground for learning, adaptation, and shared strategies to enhance global practices.
2. Threats and Economic Costs

   Mismanaged waste, notably single-use plastics (SUPs) and food waste not only poses significant threats to environmental and human health via pollution and GHG emissions but also entails substantial economic costs pertaining to inefficient resource utilization, lost recycling opportunities, and escalated disposal costs. Comparative analysis underlines the urgent need for policies that balance environmental protection with economic feasibility to foster a circular economy.

3. Collaborative Policy Solutions
   Through comparative policy review, the report highlights innovative solutions, emphasizing the critical role of transnational collaboration in combating waste management challenges. Innovative policies, especially those targeting SUPs reduction and food waste management, reflect both countries' potential to lead global waste management improvements through shared practices and policy adaptations.

Policy Recommendations

Despite current geopolitical tensions, the potential for U.S.-China cooperation in addressing critical waste management challenges remains immense. By harnessing their collective strengths, sharing innovations, and fostering an environment of mutual learning and cooperation, both countries can significantly contribute to mitigating the effects of climate change, advancing sustainable waste management practices, and moving towards a more sustainable and circular global economy.

To leverage the strengths and mitigate the weaknesses of both nations' waste management strategies, the report proposes a series of policy recommendations aimed at fostering collaboration and driving mutual and global improvements. Recommendations focus on enhancing GHG emission reductions, especially methane from landfills; incentivizing plastic recycling; managing food waste more effectively; integrating waste management into broader U.S.-China climate cooperation; and supporting multilateral exchanges and technology transfers.

Introduction

The Earth is currently facing a critical juncture in its environmental health, grappling with a "triple planetary crisis": climate change, significant biodiversity loss, and an alarming increase in pollution levels. This crisis manifests through intensifying heatwaves, more frequent and severe precipitation events, the expansion of contaminated territories, deteriorating air quality, and the proliferation of marine debris. Pollution, a longstanding adversary, exerts profound pressures on both human well-being and global ecosystems. Waste pollution, in particular, demands immediate attention due to its far-reaching implications on the environment. The surge in waste production not only elevates pollutant levels but also amplifies the effects of climate change through heightened greenhouse gas emissions. Additionally, the ecological devastation wrought by pollutants has precipitated considerable declines in natural habitats, with plastic and food waste emerging as particularly acute areas of concern.

In the contemporary context, effective waste management is imperative for environmental preservation and the promotion of sustainable development. The explosion in global population numbers, coupled with rapid urban expansion, has significantly increased the volume of solid waste generated. The World Bank's "Solid Waste

Management" report[1] estimates that the world annually produces approximately 2.01 billion metric tons of municipal solid waste, a figure projected to swell to 3.4 billion metric tons by 2050. Notably, there is a positive linkage between waste generation and income levels, with affluent nations expected to see a 19% rise in per capita waste production by 2050. Conversely, low and middle-income countries might experience over a 40% uptick. The burgeoning urban waste dilemma poses significant challenges to sustainable city management, resource efficiency, and public health.

Addressing this issue necessitates a paradigm shift towards a green and circular economy that encourages globally sustainable production and consumption practices. The pivotal role of solid waste management in this transition necessitates an ecological efficiency assessment that incorporates both environmental and economic considerations. From an economic standpoint, streamlined waste management practices not only diminish disposal expenditures but also spur employment and economic activities within the recycling sector. Although rigorous waste categorization and proper disposal entail considerable financial investment, the accrued benefits to societal welfare, environmental health, and human quality of life are substantial. The circular economy model does more than just fulfil environmental conservation and resource optimization criteria; it also engenders lucrative opportunities for businesses and individuals alike, thereby establishing a robust economic framework conducive to sustainable development, environmental stewardship, and the advancement of ecological civilization.

Nevertheless, disparities in how municipal waste is managed are evident across different economic development spectrums, notably between developed nations like the United States and emerging economies such as China. In an effort to mitigate waste generation, China has embarked on initiatives to create "zero-waste cities," enforcing stringent waste segregation laws and focusing on enhancing recycling rates—from imposing plastic mitigating restrictions in 2020 and Waste Import Ban in 2017. Meanwhile, the United States, traditionally dependent on landfilling of municipal solid waste, is gradually shifting towards more sustainable materials management strategies. This shift aims to reconcile conventional disposal methods with innovative, eco-friendly alternatives, including recycling and new technological solutions. However, both nations encounter obstacles in elevating environmental consciousness among the populace, fostering public engagement in ecological initiatives, and modernizing waste management infrastructures to accommodate current and future demands.

[1] World Bank. "Solid Waste Management." 2018. Accessed January 20, 2024.http://www.worldbank.org/en/topic/urbandevelopment/brief/solid-waste-management.

Contents

Introduction of Main Contributors

Haifeng Huang is a Fellow of the China Environment Forum at the Woodrow Wilson International Center for Scholars, an Associate Member of the Club of Rome, and served as a Board Member (2020–2023) of the UNGC PRME Steering Committee and as a National Supervisory Commissioner at the Ministry of Natural Resources of the People's Republic of China (2010–2020). He currently serves as Senior Advisor at the School of Environment and Energy, Peking University Shenzhen Graduate School, and at the Zigen Fund. He is the Co-Founder and Executive Chair of the Ecological Development Union International (EDUI) and holds the position of Distinguished Professor and Co-Chancellor at the China Institute for Responsible Management Education and Sustainable Development at Changzhou University. Dr. Huang has held full-time professorial roles at Peking University (2011–2020) and Beijing University of Technology (2002–2011). An accomplished author, he has published over ten books on sustainable development, business ethics, waste management, and the recycling economy. His book, *Recycling Economy in Germany*, received national honors and significantly contributed to the enactment of the Recycling Economy Promotion Law in China in 2008. In 2009, his proposal, "The Comprehensive Implementation of Waste Classification," won the Most Influential Proposal Award in Beijing. Dr. Huang earned his Ph.D. from Humboldt University of Berlin in Germany in 2000.

Samuel O. Idowu is Professor of Accounting and Sustainability at the Guildhall School of Business and Law, London Metropolitan University where he is currently the course leader for the MSc Corporate Social Responsibility & Sustainability and Advanced Diploma in Professional Development (ADPD) Corporate Social Responsibility & Sustainability. Samuel is also a Professor of CSR and Sustainability at Nanjing University of Finance & Economics, China. He is a fellow member of the Chartered Governance Institute, a fellow of the Royal Society of Arts, a Liveryman of the Worshipful Company of Chartered Governance Institute and a named freeman of the City of London. He is the CEO and President of the Global Corporate Governance Institute, an international network of CSR scholars. Samuel has published over one hundred articles in both professional and academic journals and contributed chapters in several edited books and is the Editor-in-Chief of three major global reference books by Springer—the *Encyclopedia of Corporate Social Responsibility* (ECSR), the *Dictionary of Corporate Social Responsibility* (DCSR) and the *Encyclopedia of Sustainable Management* (ESM) and he is a Series Editor for Springer's CSR, Sustainability, Ethics and Governance books. Samuel is the Editor-in-Chief of the *International Journal of Corporate Social Responsibility* and the *American Journal of Economics and Business Administration.* Samuel has been in academia for more than 30 years winning one of the Highly Commended Awards of Emerald Literati Network Awards for Excellence in 2008 and 2014. In 2010, one of his edited books was placed in 18th position out of forty top Sustainability books by Cambridge University Programme for Sustainability Leadership and in 2016 one of his books won the outstanding Business Reference Book of the year of the American Library Association. In 2018 he won a CSR Leadership Award in Cologne, Germany and in 2019 he won the 101 Most Impactful CSR Leaders Award in Mumbai, India. Samuel is on the Editorial Advisory Boards of the *International Journal of Business Administration.* He has been researching in the field of CSR since 1983 and has attended and presented papers at several national and international conferences and workshops on CSR. Samuel has made a number of keynote speeches at international conferences and workshops and written the *foreword* to a number of leading books in the field of CSR and Sustainable Development. And he has examined on a few PhD theses in the UK, Australia, South Africa, the Netherlands and New Zealand.

Hao Sun is a Tenure-Track Assistant Professor at Gallaudet University's School of Civic Leadership, Business, and Social Change. He also serves as an Adjunct Professor at American University's School of Public Affairs and a Visiting Research Fellow at the Langston University Center for Rehabilitation Research and Training. His professional experiences include working as a Senior Research Analyst at the Brookings Institution's Center for Technology Innovation and Race, Prosperity, and Inclusion Initiative (RPI), as well as with major media outlets like China Central Television (CCTV) and Cable News Network (CNN). Dr. Sun's academic work has been published in journals such as *Public Management Review*, *The World Economy*, and *Global Economy Journal.* His research has been cited by the Federal Reserve Board, the Society of Actuaries, *The New York Times*, *The Washington Post*, and other leading media outlets. He holds a Master's degree in Economics from Central Michigan University, a Master's degree in Political Science from the Maxwell School of Citizenship and Public Affairs at Syracuse University, and a Ph.D. in Public Administration from the Rockefeller College of Public Affairs & Policy at the State University of New York (SUNY).

Chuanbing Zhou is a Research Fellow at Research Center for Eco-Environmental Sciences, Chinese Academy of Sciences, PI of the research group Urban Metabolism and Industrial Ecology, Director of the Technical Commission of Ecological Health, Chinese Society of Ecology. The research interests are urban metabolism, food and plastic waste recycling, eco-remediation of landfills.

Yang Li is a research scholar at the University of California, Berkeley. His research focuses on ESG, responsible business, and environmental impact. He holds a Master of Science in Computer Applied Technology from Peking University.

Rocco Cartusciello is the Research Assistant to Professor Haifeng Huang at the Wilson Center's China Environmental Forum. His research focuses on Southeast Asian Affairs and Foreign Policy. He holds a Master's Degree in Asian Studies from Georgetown University.

Zhangchen Wang is a Research Assistant at the Institute for China-America Studies. His research focuses on climate change policy, sustainable development, and security policies. He holds a Masters of Arts degree in International Relations from Johns Hopkins University.

Yuhang Sun is a Ph.D. Candidate at the City University of Hong Kong. His research focuses on sustainable development. He graduated from Peking University with a Master degree in Environmental Science.

Simon Choi LLB (Peking), LLM (London), PhD (Malaya), Linguist (UK) & Solicitor (England & Wales). A visiting professor of the School of Transnational School, Peking University, Legal Advisor of Ecological Development Union International, and General Counsel of the Global Legal Centre of Guangdong Liangma Law Firm. His research focuses on ESG, green finance and fintech law.

Di Wu is serving as executive secretary general of Ecological Development Union International in China. He holds a Master of Management from Peking University. He focuses on green finance, enterprise management and SDG.

Jiayu Deng is serving as the General Secretary of the Fujian Green Home Environmental Protection Center, concurrently holds the position of Director at the Environmental Public Welfare Law Clinic of Yango University. She holds a Master of Environmental Law and Policy from Vermont Law School. She focuses on international climate change law, sustainable development research, local environmental governance and policymaking, and carbon taxation.

Xavier Zheng is an Associate at RMI. He focuses on reforming utility business models using performance-based regulation. Prior to this role, he interned at the Wilson Center, where he gained valuable experience in energy policy analysis and research. He holds a Master of Arts degree in International Relations from Johns Hopkins University.

Li Pan is graduated from Nanjing University of Aeronautics and Astronautics with a Master degree in Law. His research focuses on the intersection of economic challenges and administrative policies.

Qi Chen is a master candidate at Nanjing University of Finance & Economics. His research focuses on ESG and Corporate Social Responsibility.

Tongshang Li is Research Assistant at the Institute for China-America Studies. She is a bachelor candidate at Sichuan Normal University. Her research focuses on Chinese climate change policy.

Zichong Ye is a master candidate at Johns Hopkins SAIS. His research focuses on climate politics, green protectionism, and China's overseas investment. He holds a B.A. in International Affairs from The George Washington University.

Zhuoyi Liu is served as a research assistant intern at the Wilson Center. He is a master candidate in Foreign Service at Georgetown University's School of Foreign Service. His research focuses on energy and various sustainable project investment, green policy, supply chain, and business innovations.

Chunni Song is a master candidate in International Relations at Johns Hopkins SAIS. Her research focuses on climate change, green energy transition and sustainable development. She holds a Bachelor degree in International Affairs from the George Washington University.

List of Figures

List of Tables

Chapter 1
Comparative Analysis of Urban Waste Management Trends in the US and China

1.1 Summary

Municipal Solid Waste (MSW) poses significant environmental challenges for urban areas, particularly in the world's largest producers: the United States and China. This section explores and examines trends in waste generation, management approaches, and the environmental, health, and economic impacts of waste in these two countries.

1.1.1 Trends in Waste Generation

In 2018, the US generated 266 million tons of MSW, surpassing China's 212 million tons. Single-use plastics (SUPs) and food waste are major contributors, with China producing 25.4 million metric tons of SUP waste in 2019, followed by the US at 17.2 million metric tons. By 2021, the global SUP production from virgin fossil fuels rose to 137 million metric tons (MMT), highlighting the need for a circular economy. Food waste significantly contributes to greenhouse gas emissions, due to the landfilling and composting processes.

1.1.2 Waste Management Approaches

Waste management strategies reveal similarities and differences in the U.S. and China. Both countries primarily use landfills for plastic waste. China's recycling rates have increased, though incineration and poor management persist. In contrast, the U.S. shows slower recycling growth but fewer issues with incineration and mismanagement.

H. Huang et al., *Waste Management for Global Sustainability*, CSR, Sustainability, Ethics & Governance, https://doi.org/10.1007/978-981-96-8305-5_1

Regarding food waste, over half of the US's waste was landfilled in 2018, with the remainder treated via incineration, composting, and other methods.[1] China's approach has shifted towards incineration and composting, aiming for "zero landfill" for the developed cities in eastern and middle China.[2]

1.1.3 Environmental and Health Impacts

Plastic and food waste pose severe environmental threats. Plastics resist degradation, contaminating soil and water. Untreated food waste can produce odors, breeding pests, and further degrade soil. Health risks associated with waste include respiratory, digestive, and reproductive issues from incinerating plastic waste, and foodborne illnesses from pathogens in mismanaged food waste. Additionally, waste disposal processes significantly contribute to greenhouse gas emissions, worsening climate change by the effluxes of methane and nitrous oxide.

1.1.4 Economic and Policy Considerations

Economic costs of municipal solid waste management are high, with global food waste exceeding 1 trillion USD annually. Effective waste management is economically essential, requiring investments in recycling infrastructure, sustainable practices, and strict policy implementation. International collaboration is crucial to address these challenges and achieve sustainable urban waste management.

The US and China must adopt comprehensive waste management strategies that emphasize prevention, reduction, reuse, and recycling. Addressing the environmental and health impacts through innovative solutions and policy reforms is vital for mitigating waste's detrimental effects, paving the way for a sustainable future.

[1] U.S. Environmental Protection Agency, "United States 2030 Food Loss and Waste Reduction Goal," https://www.epa.gov/sustainable-management-food/united-states-2030-food-loss-and-waste-reduction-goal.

[2] Marco Raugei, "Net Energy Analysis Must Not Compare Apples and Oranges," *Clean Energy* 4, no. 3 (2020): 169–178, https://academic.oup.com/ce/article/4/3/169/5918339?login=false.

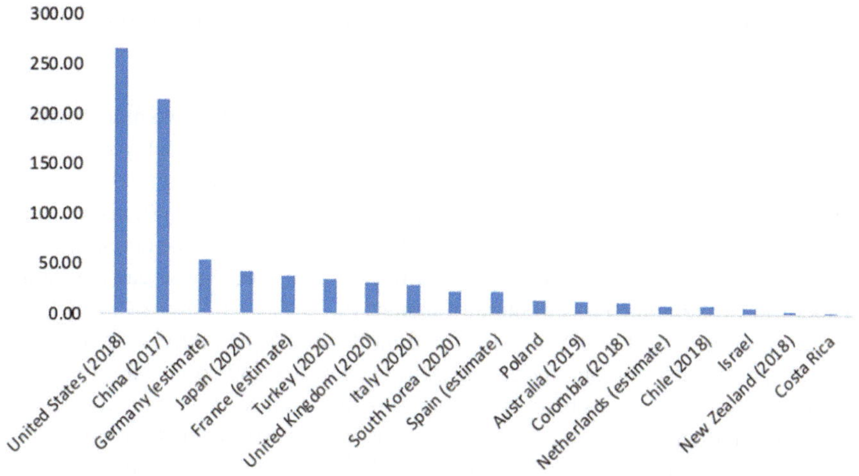

Fig. 1.1 Generation of municipal waste as of 2021 (in million metric tons) (*Source* OECD Database)

1.2 Comparative Analysis of Urban Waste Management Trends in the US and China

1.2.1 Trends in the Types and Amount of Waste Generated in Both Countries

1.2.1.1 Volume of Municipal Solid Waste (MSW) Produced in Each Country

The United States and China stand as the two predominant producers of Municipal Solid Waste (MSW) globally. Defined as solid or semi-solid waste originating from households, commercial venues, and institutions, MSW presents considerable environmental challenges.[3] In the year 2018, China was responsible for producing around 212 million tons of MSW, whereas the United States exceeded this with an approximate generation of 266 million tons of MSW (Fig. 1.1).

[3] S. Sikder, S. M. Toha, and M. Mostafizur Rahman, "An Overview on Municipal Solid Waste Characteristics and Its Impacts on Environment and Human Health," in *Technical Landfills and Waste Management: Volume 1: Landfill Impacts, Characterization, and Valorisation* (OECD Stat. Extracts. Online database; 2024).

1.2.1.2 Composition of Municipal Solid Waste (MSW) Types in Both Nations

Among the generated MSW, plastic waste and food waste are the two major components that account for a significant proportion of the waste stream. Each year, humans produce 430 million tons of plastic, of which approximately 70% quickly becomes waste. Around 23 million tons of plastic directly enter aquatic ecosystems, posing a direct threat to the health of these systems. Moreover, throughout the entire lifecycle of plastics, they contribute to nearly one-fifth of global greenhouse gas emissions, further exacerbating the risks of climate change.

The composition of MSW in China and the United States differs significantly. However, before delving into the specific differences in MSW composition between the two countries, it is worth mentioning that the Chinese government needs to further strengthen its statistical analysis of MSW composition nationwide. Upon reviewing the current Chinese government archives regarding MSW management, it is evident that there are certain variations in how MSW composition is presented across different cities and regions in China. Therefore, this report relies on data on Chinese urban solid waste composition analyzed by Chinese scholars using machine learning algorithms. This data can be considered relatively authoritative in terms of analyzing the composition of solid waste in China. Additionally, this data also provides insights into the changing characteristics of MSW composition in China, facilitating further analysis of the evolution of MSW composition in the country.

Overall, it can be observed that in China, organic waste constitutes the majority of MSW, accounting for over 50% of the composition. Additionally, plastics and paper also make up a significant proportion of China's MSW composition. In contrast, for the United States, based on the data we have collected, official statistics published by the Environmental Protection Agency (EPA) provide a detailed analysis of the annual composition of MSW in the country. From these statistics, it is evident that the U.S. government has accumulated considerable experience and historical data in collecting basic information on MSW. In terms of MSW composition in the United States, paper waste has the largest share, followed by food waste, plastic waste, and yard waste. This partly reflects the need for further consideration on reducing and recycling food and plastic waste in the U.S. MSW management efforts (Figs. 1.2 and 1.3).

1.2.1.3 Concerns with Single-Use Plastics (SUPs) and Food Waste

In 2019, there were 131 million metric tons (MMT) of single-use plastics made from virgin fossil-fuel-based polymers, while only 1.7 MMT of single-use plastics were produced from recycled feedstocks. By 2021, the global production of single-use plastics made from virgin fossil-fuel-based polymers increased to 137 MMT, representing a 6 MMT increase compared to 2019. However, in 2021, the production of single-use plastics made from recycled feedstocks remained low at only 2.1 MMT, with a mere 0.4 MMT increase compared to 2019. It is estimated that by 2027,

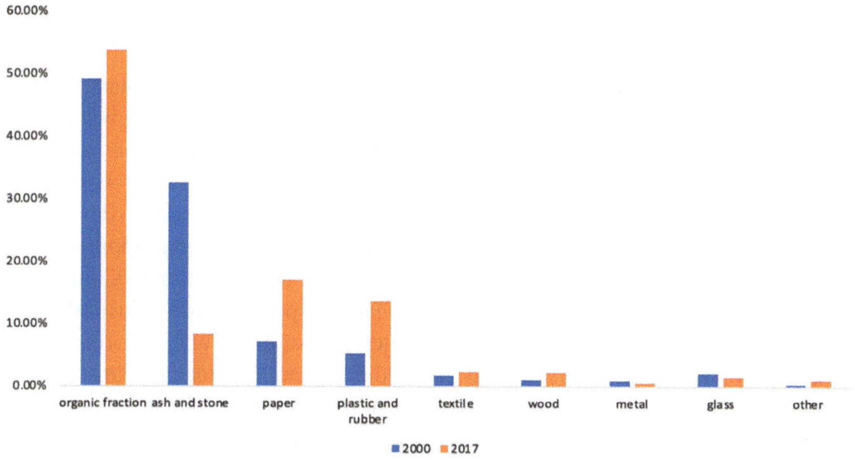

Fig. 1.2 Estimating physical composition of MSW in China (*Source* [Shijun Ma et al., 2020])

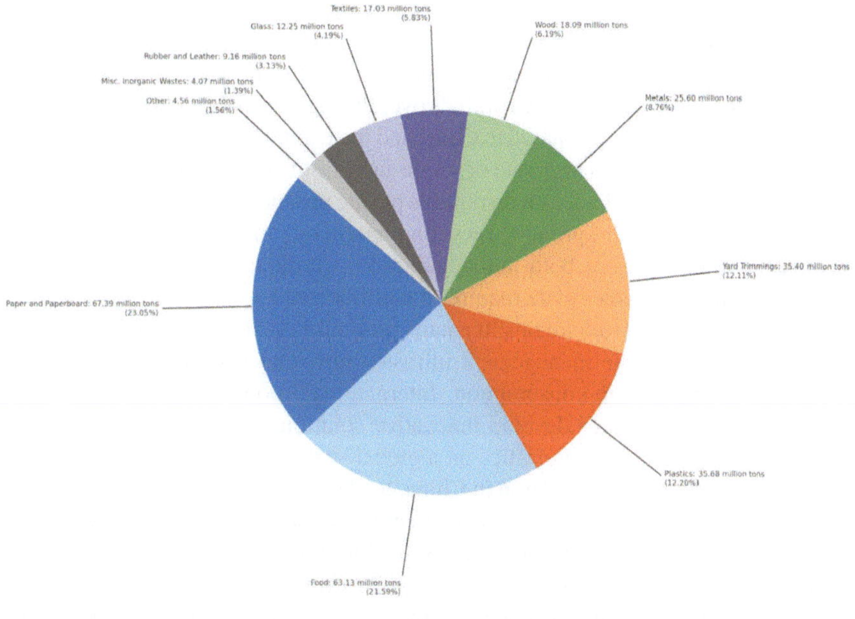

Fig. 1.3 Municipal solid waste generated by material, 2018 (in million tons)

the annual global production of single-use plastics made from virgin fossil-fuel-based polymers will reach 148 MMT, while the production of single-use plastics made from recycled feedstocks will only reach 4.7 MMT. The majority of single-use plastic products globally continue to be manufactured from virgin fossil-fuel sources, highlighting the urgent need to promote a circular economy in the production and processing of single-use plastics.

In 2019, China emerged as the largest generator of single-use plastic waste, producing a staggering 25.4 million metric tons.[4] Following closely behind was the United States, which generated an estimated 17.2 million metric tons of single-use plastic waste. While Australia's net generation of single-use plastic waste in the same year was comparatively lower, at 1.5 million metric tons, it exhibited one of the highest rates of single-use plastic waste generation per capita, with approximately 59 kg per person. These figures highlight the significant contribution of China to the global single-use plastic waste crisis. With its large population and industrial development, the country faces immense challenges in managing and reducing plastic waste. Efforts to address this issue have gained momentum in recent years, with the Chinese government implementing measures to restrict the production and use of single-use plastics. These include bans on non-biodegradable plastic bags, disposable straws, and foam containers in various cities. In the United States, the substantial volume of single-use plastic waste underscores the need for enhanced waste management strategies and a shift toward more sustainable alternatives. Several states and cities have taken measures to reduce plastic waste, such as imposing plastic bag fees, promoting recycling programs, and encouraging the use of reusable products. However, there is still much room for improvement in terms of nationwide policies and consumer behavior. While Australia's overall single-use plastic waste generation appears relatively lower compared to China and the United States, its per capita rate is concerning. The country's high rate of single-use plastic waste generation per person indicates a significant reliance on disposable plastic products. This calls for concerted efforts to raise awareness, promote recycling initiatives, and encourage the adoption of reusable alternatives at both individual and institutional levels. Addressing the issue of single-use plastic waste requires a multifaceted approach involving governments, businesses, and individuals. It entails promoting sustainable production practices, investing in waste management infrastructure, and fostering a cultural shift towards reducing plastic consumption. International cooperation and knowledge-sharing are also crucial to develop innovative solutions and mitigate the environmental impact of single-use plastics on a global scale. By recognizing the scale of single-use plastic waste generation in China, the United States, and Australia, stakeholders can work together to implement effective measures that reduce plastic waste, protect ecosystems, and create a more sustainable future (Fig. 1.4).

In 2021, the cradle-to-grave (Scope 1, 2, and 3) greenhouse gas (GHG) emissions resulting from the life cycle of single-use plastics were estimated to be approximately 450 million metric tons (MMT) of CO_2 equivalent. This staggering amount exceeds the total GHG emissions of the United Kingdom. It highlights the significant contribution of single-use plastics to the global carbon footprint and emphasizes the urgent need for sustainable alternatives and improved waste management practices. These findings underscore the critical role that addressing single-use plastic emissions plays in mitigating climate change and achieving global climate targets. Efforts to reduce

[4] D. Charles and L. Kimman, "Plastic Waste Makers Index 2021.".

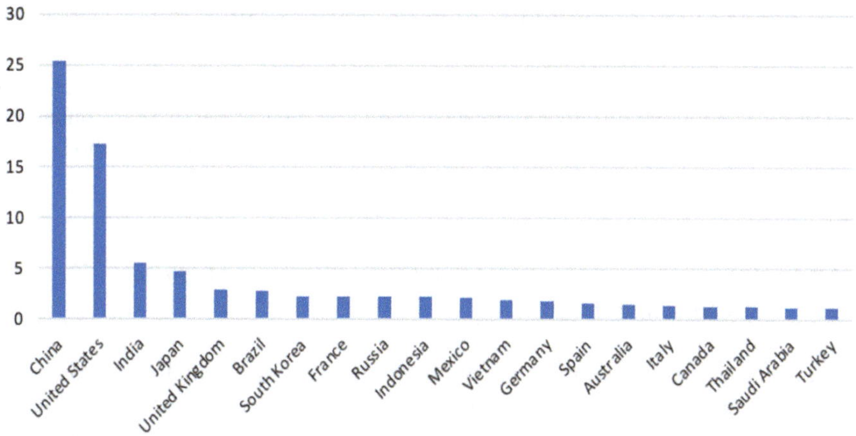

Fig. 1.4 Largest single-use plastic waste generating countries worldwide in 2019 (in million metric tons) (*Source* The plastic waste makers index, 2021)

single-use plastic consumption, promote recycling and circular economy practices, and transition to more sustainable materials are crucial in curbing these emissions and minimizing their environmental impact.

As for the food waste issue, food waste is the world's third-largest source of greenhouse gas emissions, with only China and the United States emitting more. According to a study by Poore and Nemecek, the majority of food waste, approximately 91%, is generated during production, storage, and processing due to poor storage and handling techniques, lack of refrigeration, and spoilage during transportation and processing. In contrast, consumer waste accounts for only 9% of the total.[5] This estimation is based on data from 2018 and does not include food losses on farms during production and harvesting, suggesting that greenhouse gas emissions from food waste are likely even higher. From this perspective, the greenhouse gas emissions from food waste are equivalent to the global aviation sector emissions. Comparing food waste emissions to national emissions, it would rank as the third-largest emitter behind only China (21%) and the United States (13%).

1.2.2 *Threats to Human and Environmental Health from Solid Waste Pollution and Greenhouse Gas Emissions*

Globally, the United Nations Environment Programme *Global Waste Management Outlook* emphasizes the importance of comprehensive waste management strategies

[5] J. Poore and T. Nemecek, "Reducing Food's Environmental Impacts Through Producers and Consumers," *Science* 360, no. 6392 (2018): 987–992.

for sustainable development and climate change mitigation. Waste disposal for plastic and food waste is mainly through uncontrolled dumping, open burning and landfills.[6] However, these waste disposal methods vary greatly among countries, with China and the U.S. adopting different approaches based on their respective environmental policies and technological advances, and the different waste disposal methods have different levels of impact on the environment as well as human health.

1.2.2.1 Comparison of Municipal Solid Waste Disposal Methods in China and the U.S.

A waste management hierarchy based on the most environmentally friendly principles prioritizes waste prevention and reduction, followed by waste reuse, recycling and composting. In many countries, however, the main options for disposal are currently burying these wastes in landfills and incineration.

China and the U.S. show partial consistency in waste disposal strategies, as well as significant differences. The combined data on plastic and food waste disposal in municipal waste show that in recent years, both China and the United States have dominated plastic waste disposal in the form of landfills, which has always been the mainstay of plastic waste disposal in China and the United States. In recent years, China's recycling volume has grown significantly, but incineration and poor management still account for a large portion of the waste. In contrast, the U.S. has a lower incineration and mismanagement share of waste, but a slower growth rate in recycling (Table 1.1).

Adapted from (Technology leader, 2020; Solid Waste observation public account, 2022; Jiacheng, 2023; Weber Consulting, 2020; Yu et al., 2023; Economic reference network, 2019; Michael et al. 2017) (Figs. 1.5 and 1.6).

In 2018, the U.S. Environmental Protection Agency (EPA) estimated that the total amount of food wasted in the United States was 57.27 million tons. More than half of the waste is disposed of in landfills, and the rest is decomposed and recycled by incineration, composting and other means.[7] In 2020, 50.3% of China's food waste was treated by landfills, 38.2% by incineration, and the rest by aerobic composting or anaerobic digestion.[8] In recent years, with the implementation and promotion of the goal of "zero landfill" of raw domestic waste by 2023, the proportion of landfill treatment in the urban domestic waste treatment structure has been decreasing year by year. However, as the amount of food waste generated continues to grow, there is still a gap in low-carbon and sustainable waste disposal methods and capacity.

---

[6] United Nations Environment Programme, *Global Waste Management Outlook*, https://www.unep.org/resources/report/global-waste-management-outlook.

[7] Greenpeace, "A Low-Carbon Code for Kitchen Waste," accessed February 27, 2024, https://www.greenpeace.org.cn/food-waste/.

[8] Kirsten J., et al., "From Farm to Kitchen: The Environmental Impacts of U.S. Food Waste," U.S. Environmental Protection Agency Office of Research and Development, accessed March 21, 2024, https://www.epa.gov/land-research/farm-kitchen-environmental-impacts-us-food-waste.

Table 1.1 Comparative analysis of urban waste management trends in the US and China

Methods	China	United States
Landfilling and open dumping	High landfill volume; insufficient land resources; classified landfills	Large landfill volume; abundant land resources; advanced containment systems
Incineration	High rates and increased number of incineration plants; Government-mandated 'Waste Segregation'; Overcapacity of incineration plants; Two kinds of incineration energy production technology: grate furnace & cement kiln co-generation	Low rates and number of plants; Widespread opposition from citizens and organizations
Recycling	Government-regulated; weak management; advanced sorting devices	Weakly regulated; services by private/ government organizations; advanced sorting
Mismanagement	High-levels; food waste issues	Stricter regulations; issues with improper disposal and illegal transportation

1.2.2.2 Threats to the Environment and Human Beings Posed by Plastic and Food Waste

As one of the major environmental problems facing the world, municipal waste such as plastic and food poses a great threat to human beings and ecosystems.

Plastic waste and food waste pose a serious threat to the environment, damaging soil quality and reducing the efficiency of resource recovery. Plastic waste, especially single-use plastics, is inherently difficult to degrade. The use of landfill technology to dispose of this type of waste consumes large areas of land resources, limiting the potential utilization of the land, while at the same time releasing chemicals such as additives from decomposition that can cause soil contamination problems. The accumulation of microplastics can cause the soil to become compacted, reducing its air and water circulation, which negatively affects the root growth of plants and their overall development. Additionally, when microplastics accumulate on the surface of plants, they also hinder their growth and ability to photosynthesize. Compared to plastics, which are difficult to decompose naturally, food waste decomposes faster, but

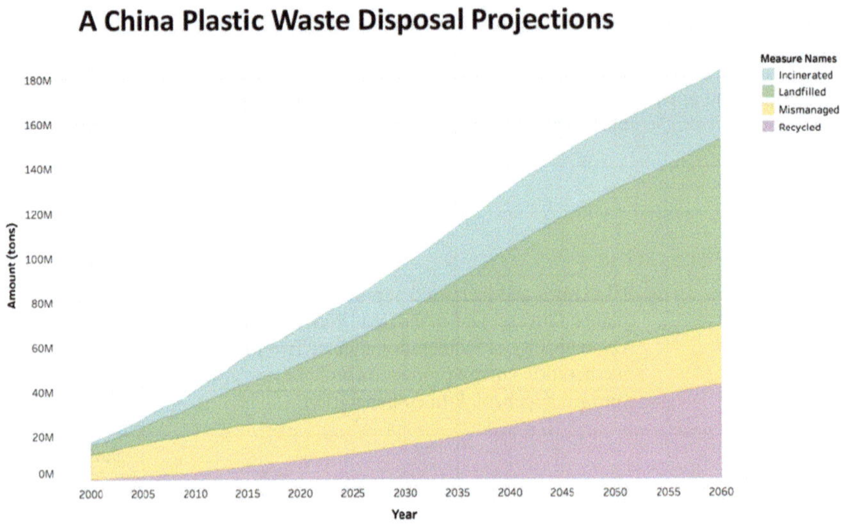

Fig. 1.5 A China plastic waste disposal projections

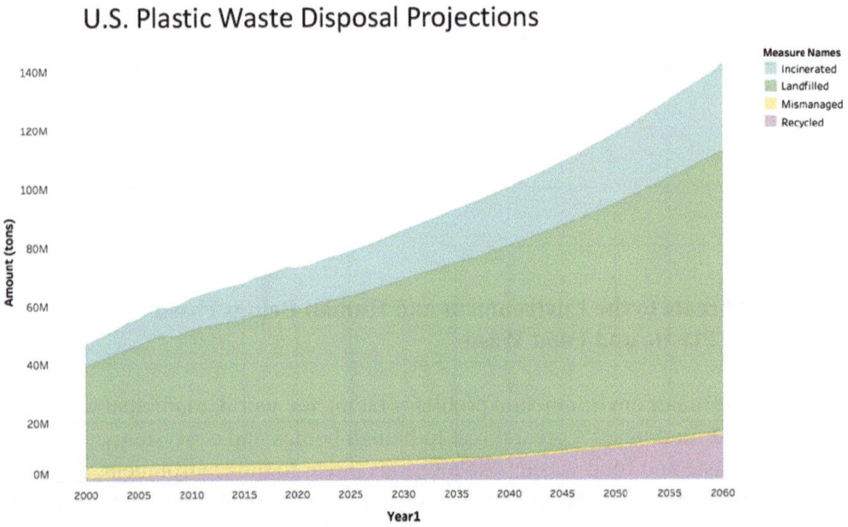

Fig. 1.6 B U.S. Plastic waste disposal projections (*Source* Our world in data)

the high water content, high organic content, and high oil, grease and salt content of these wastes increase the difficulty of treatment and significantly reduce the efficiency of resource recycling. If improperly handled or stored for treatment, food waste tends to emit unpleasant odors and may also become a breeding ground for pathogenic microorganisms, reducing soil fertility and exacerbating land pressure.

Plastics and food waste pose a multifaceted threat to human health, including not only triggering a variety of problems in the respiratory, digestive and reproductive systems, but also potential disease-causing risks. Different types of plastics have different levels of impact on human systems. For example, polyvinyl chloride may cause health problems including chronic bronchitis, skin problems, deafness, heart failure, digestive problems, and liver damage. PS (polystyrene) may irritate the eyes, nose, and throat, cause dizziness and coma, migrate to food and accumulate in body fat, and may increase the risk of cancers of the lymphatic and hematopoietic systems.[9] Food waste contains a large number of bacteria and viruses such as Salmonella, E. coli, and norovirus. These pathogens can spread through contact or consumption of contaminated food, causing food poisoning, diarrhea, vomiting and other digestive diseases.

Gasses released from plastics and food waste disposal contribute significantly to the greenhouse effect. In 2019, plastics produced 1.8 billion metric tons of greenhouse gas emissions (carbon dioxide from fossil carbon combustion) - 3.4% of global GHG emissions. Plastics produced 1.9 billion greenhouse gasses, as well as other chemicals such as sulfur compounds, which contribute to environmental challenges such as acid rain, increased greenhouse effect, and ozone layer damage.[10] Disposable plastics account for a staggering 91% of all plastic products. The high stability of traditional single-use plastics such as polyethylene (PE), polypropylene (PP), and polyvinyl chloride (PVC) is difficult to decompose completely in the natural environment, and although pyrolysis provides a highly efficient treatment method to dispose of single-use plastics, the real process is energy intensive, and the quality and quantity of energy recovered from pyrolysis (e.g., oil) may not be sufficient to offset the process energy consumption, affecting the overall energy efficiency.[11] At the same time, harmful gasses and other by-products such as carbon dioxide, carbon monoxide, and sulfur compounds may be produced during the pyrolysis process, increasing air pollution.

Disposal of municipal waste such as plastics and food can also seriously threaten the normal functioning of aquatic ecosystems. Residues left over from the decomposition of plastics are transformed by natural processes into tiny microplastic or nanoplastic particles. These tiny particles are easily driven by water currents due to their large surface area and end up in the oceans. When microplastics or large untreated plastics are accidentally ingested by aquatic organisms, they accumulate in the body and can lead to asphyxiation, intestinal blockage and even death. In addition to this, plastic waste may also affect human health along the food chain after being consumed by humans through marine organisms. Food waste, which is rich in higher nutrients, and the overflow of garbage leachate during treatment contain high concentrations of organic matter, nitrogen, phosphorus and other nutrients, which, if

[9] Z. Sineng, et al., "Microplastics in the Environment and Their Effects on Human Health," *China Plastics* 33, no. 4 (2019): 81–88.

[10] Hannah Ritchie and Max Roser, "Greenhouse Gas Emissions from Plastics," *Our World in Data*, accessed August 7, 2024, https://ourworldindata.org/ghg-emissions-plastics.

[11] H. Shilei and F. Zong, "Treatment Methods and Development Trend of Waste Biodegradable Plastics," *China Environmental Science* 43, no. 12 (2023): 6445–6464.

discharged directly without treatment, can lead to eutrophication of the water body, affecting the quality of water and the health of aquatic organisms. In order to effectively solve these problems, the treatment technology of food waste has gradually developed towards harmlessness and resourcefulness. Through the bioconversion and recycling of important elements such as carbon, nitrogen, phosphorus and potassium in food waste, these substances can be converted into new resources.

Plastic and food waste discharged directly into ecosystems without proper treatment poses significant environmental and public health risks, interfering with ecological balance and potentially causing a range of human health problems. Approximately 25% of global plastic waste is either improperly handled or leaked into the natural environment. This represents about 82 million tons of waste that isn't securely disposed of in landfills, recycled, or burned. Food waste, if not disposed of in a timely manner, attracts and aids propagation of pests and animals such as rats and flies, which can carry diseases and spread them to humans through contact or the food chain, increasing the risk of infectious diseases. The oils, fats and chemicals in them can lead to the accumulation of harmful substances in soil and water bodies, reducing the quality of the soil in which crops are grown and contaminating groundwater. At the same time, the direct disposal of untreated food waste means that the organic matter and nutrients in it cannot be recycled, resulting in a significant waste of energy and resources (Tables 1.2 and 1.3).

Table 1.2 Threats from Single Use Plastics (SUPs) (page 35)

Threats	Effects of SUPs
Degradation of Land	Increases landfill capacity issues, leading to land use issues; leeches harmful chemicals and plastic debris into soil and groundwater, reducing fertility and contaminating crops
Harm to Human Health	Breaks down into microplastics (under photolysis) that enter the food chain, causing health issues like endocrine disruption and toxicity; incineration releases toxic smoke and particulate matter, affecting respiratory health
Influence of Aquatic Ecosystem	Major contributor to ocean pollution; significant water use for recycling processes; plastics accumulate in aquatic organisms, causing physical harm, blockages, and death; disrupts marine ecosystems and food webs; exacerbates pressure on water-scarce regions due to high water consumption in production and recycling; microplastics ingested by marine mammals, birds, and other wildlife, causing injury, poisoning, and mortality; disrupts natural habitats and biodiversity
Climate Change	Significant greenhouse gas emissions from the production of plastics (CO_2, CH_4, N_2O); incineration of plastics releases CO_2 and other pollutants; energy-intensive processes add to the carbon footprint, contributing to global warming and climate change

Source Adapted from (Landwall 2020; Preeti, 2023; Brad, 2023)

Table 1.3 Land and waste management (page 36)

Threats	Food Production Process	Food Disposal Process—Management	Food Disposal Process—Mismanagement
Degradation of Land	Excessive land cultivation and grazing lead to soil degradation and habitat loss	Landfill leachate contaminates soil, reducing fertility and intensifying land use pressure	Limits land use potential, leading to soil structure and quality deterioration
Waste of Natural Resources	High usage of water, energy, and fertilizer; 21% of freshwater, 19% of fertilizer, and 18% of arable land contribute to landfill waste	Overflowing landfill leachate pollutes freshwater resources with high concentrations of nutrients and organic matter; Untreated landfill leachate affects water quality, leading to eutrophication and harming aquatic organisms	Pollutants from mismanaged waste enter water bodies, causing water quality deterioration and loss of biodiversity, disrupting the water cycle
Harm to Biodiversity	Conversion of natural ecosystems to agriculture reduces habitat quality and biodiversity		
Climate Change	High greenhouse gas emissions from food production, including CO_2 from fuel and fertilizer use, and methane from livestock	GHGs from food waste: CO_2, CH_4, N_2O from fuel consumption; Food waste accounts for nearly half of the global food system's GHG emissions; Methane released from rotting food, biogas from carbonaceous material; Direct emissions of mineral carbon and operational energy use; Releases CO_2, N_2O, CH_4, and NH_3; significant methane leakage; Anaerobic digestion > Aerobic compost > Incineration > Landfill	

1.2.3 Economic Costs of Plastic and Food Waste

As the process of globalization accelerates and urbanization levels continue to rise, both China and the United States, as the world's largest economies, are facing increasingly severe challenges in urban waste management. In particular, plastic and food waste not only pose a significant threat to the environment but also bring substantial economic costs. Effectively managing these wastes and reducing the economic costs of their production and disposal have become issues of common concern for governments and all sectors of society in both countries.

1.2.3.1 Analysis of the Social Costs of Plastic Waste

The disposal of plastic waste involves not only direct financial expenditures, including the costs of collection, transportation, and processing, but also indirect economic losses due to environmental pollution. The United States tends to dispose of waste through landfilling. Although landfills can immediately handle large amounts of waste without the need for complex technology and highly skilled labor, the decomposition of plastics takes a long time. During this decomposition, harmful chemicals can be released, seeping into the soil and groundwater and causing new environmental pollution. Additionally, using landfills for plastic waste means wasting plastic materials and land resources since landfills occupy significant land areas, which are difficult to revert to their original state after use. Some modern landfills capture methane gas produced during waste decomposition to generate energy, but they cannot capture 100% of the methane, meaning landfills emit a considerable amount of greenhouse gasses, exacerbating global climate change and related issues. Beyond the direct costs of waste disposal, environmental pollution leading to health problems among residents represents a substantial social cost.

The food delivery industry has become an indispensable part of people's lives. This could be understood clearly using the Meituan's delivery service as a case study. In 2022, Wen Zongguo's team conducted a first-hand research in eight typical cities—Chongqing, Beijing, Shanghai, Guangzhou, Shenzhen, Yantai, Chengdu, and Xiangyang—gathering hundreds of samples to estimate that the national takeout industry generated 1.6 million tons of plastic waste in 2020.[12] According to the data cited by Wen's team, there were 17 billion takeout orders nationwide in 2020. Meituan's financial report shows that in 2023, the total number of instant delivery orders reached 21.9 billion, most of which used plastic packaging. Although Meituan did not disclose the amount of plastic packaging used, based on the data from Professor Wen Zongguo's research, it is estimated that Meituan's delivery service generated 2.06 million tons of plastic waste in 2023.

The following will provide an approximate calculation of the social costs of plastic waste generated by Meituan's delivery service. These costs include the carbon

[12] Zhang, Yuting, and Zongguo Wen. "Mapping the Environmental Impacts and Policy Effectiveness of the Takeaway Food Industry in China." *Science of the Total Environment* 808 (2022): 152023.

emissions associated with producing takeout packaging, the expenses for collecting, transporting, and processing takeout waste, and the health impacts on people.

1.2.3.2 Carbon Emission Costs

A reasonable approach to analyze the environmental impact of a product is to conduct a life cycle assessment. For instance, the environmental pollution caused by the plastic waste from Meituan's delivery service does not only exist at the point of delivery to the customer and disposal after use. This pollution is hidden throughout the entire supply chain. To calculate the carbon emissions caused by a single use of plastic packaging in takeout, one must consider the entire life cycle of the plastic packaging, including its production, use, and disposal processes. When Wen's team assessed the impact of a single takeout order in Beijing in 2019, they found it generated 680 g of carbon emissions per food delivery order.[13] Given the differences in cities and dining habits, the carbon emissions per order may vary, but for simplicity, we assumed each order generates 680 g of carbon emissions. By this estimate, the carbon emissions associated with plastic waste from food delivery industry in 2023 amounted to 14.89 million tons. Based on the national carbon market closing price of 83.83 RMB/ton on March 21, 2024, from the Shanghai Environment and Energy Exchange, the cost of carbon emissions from Meituan's plastic packaging is approximately 1.25 billion RMB.

1.2.3.3 Harmless Disposal Costs

According to Meituan's report, "the vast majority of takeout waste enters the incineration or landfill systems with municipal waste." Therefore, we will calculate based on all plastic waste being either incinerated or landfilled. According to the 2023 Statistical Yearbook of Urban and Rural Areas, the harmless incineration rate of waste in China in 2022 was about 80%, with landfills accounting for about 12%, and other methods about 8%.[14] Since takeout is primarily concentrated in large cities where the incineration rate is higher, we will calculate based on 85% incineration and 15% landfilling. Professor Wan Junyi's team analyzed the cost of waste treatment methods in 25 cities with different levels of economic development, discussing the treatment and environmental costs associated with each method.[15]

---

[13] Wen, Zongguo, Yuting Zhang, and Daishi Fu. "Environmental Impact of a Takeaway Order Based on Whole Industry Chain Assessment." *China Environmental Science* 39, no. 9 (2019): 8.

[14] National Bureau of Statistics. *China Statistical Yearbook 2023*. Beijing: China Statistics Press, 2023. https://www.stats.gov.cn/sj/ndsj/2023/indexch.htm.

[15] Wan, Junyi, Xinru Feng, Qixu Tang, et al. "Cost-Benefit Analysis of Harmless Disposal of Municipal Solid Waste: A Case Study of 25 Cities in China." *Resources and Industries* 21, no. 4 (2019): 81–89.

Table 1.4 shows the unit cost of waste treatment for cities of different categories. Due to the higher number of takeout orders in first-tier cities and the higher incineration rate in large cities, we calculate based on 55% incineration in first-tier cities, 30% in second-tier cities, and 15% landfill in third-tier cities. Using the data from Table 1.1 and subsequent calculations, the cost of processing plastic waste generated by Meituan's delivery service in 2023 is estimated to be approximately 1.473 billion RMB. These costs include waste collection and transportation, operational and infrastructure costs, land occupation costs, and environmental pollution costs, with the latter including costs related to human health impacts (Fig. 1.7).

The social cost of plastic waste generated by Meituan's delivery service in 2023 is roughly 2.721 billion RMB. Given the difficulty in accounting for all plastic waste from takeout, this estimate of social costs is based on national estimates derived from typical sample cities selected by Wen's team. This highlights the significant social cost of plastic waste, with the hope that these data not only raise public awareness of the plastic waste issue in the takeout industry but also enhance understanding of the environmental harm caused by plastic waste.

1.2.3.4 Cost Analysis of Food Waste

Food waste is another major category of urban waste, with both China and the United States facing challenges related to food waste and its disposal. Food waste is not just a simple matter of wasting food; it also wastes the resources used to grow, store, process, distribute, and prepare the food, such as land, water, energy, and labor.

In 2022, the world wasted 1.05 billion tons of food.[16] When food waste is disposed of in landfills, it decomposes to produce methane (CH_4), a potent greenhouse gas, and landfills may also produce leachate, which can pollute the environment if it seeps into the soil untreated. Residents near landfills can be affected by air pollution, and when leachate contaminates groundwater, it can indirectly affect human health. Incinerating food waste generates carbon dioxide and other pollutants, like dioxins, which not only pollute the atmosphere but can also impact residents' health, increasing the risk of respiratory and cardiovascular diseases over long-term exposure. More than 1 trillion USD worth of food is wasted each year, and these economic costs are just the tip of the iceberg compared to the social costs mentioned above.[17]

Reducing food waste is not only an economic necessity but also a crucial path to sustainable development. Through collective efforts and innovative solutions, we can effectively reduce food waste globally, promoting economic growth, protecting the environment, and improving social welfare.

[16] United Nations Environment Programme, *Food Waste Index Report 2024. Think Eat Save: Tracking Progress to Halve Global Food Waste*, last modified March 27, 2024, accessed April 1, 2024, https://wedocs.unep.org/20.500.11822/45230.

[17] Ibid.

Table 1.4 Landfill vs incineration method (RMB/ton) (page 39)

City categories	LM—Direct net cost	LM—Environmental cost	LM—Total	IM—Direct net cost	IM—Environmental cost	IM—Total
First-tier cities	2232	26	2258	388	577	965
Second-tier cities	805	16	820	143	228	371
Third-tier cities	474	14	488	106	112	218

Source Wan Junyi (2019)

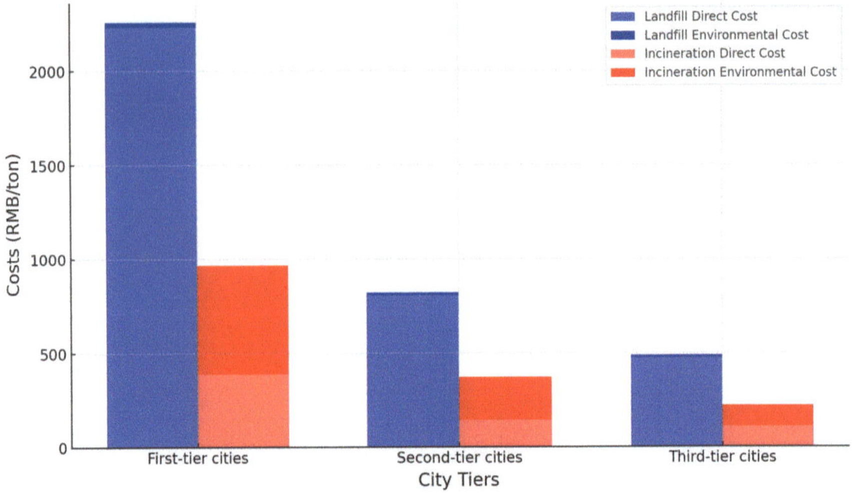

Fig. 1.7 Cost breakdown by city Tier (*Source* Wan Junyi 2019)

References

Economic Reference Network. (2019). Waste Sorting Policy Push in China. *Economic Daily*. http://www.jjckb.cn/2019-07/01/c_137281487.htm

Jiacheng, Li. "The Fourth Anniversary of Garbage Classification: The Reduction Is Successful, and the Incineration Situation Is Embarrassing." *China Dialogue*, 2023.

Landwall. (2020). China Waste-to-Energy Market Overview. *Landbell Group*. https://landbell.de/en/news/waste-toenergy- in-china/

Ma, S., Zhou, C., Chi, C., Liu, Y., & Yang, G. (2020). Estimating Physical Composition of Municipal Solid Waste in China by Applying Artificial Neural Network Method. *Environmental Science & Technology, 54*(15), 9609–9617.

Michael, N., et al. "Study on the Recovery and Utilization of Biomass Components from Municipal Solid Waste in China." Federal Ministry for the Environment, Nature Conservation, Building and Nuclear Safety, 2017.

Plumer, B. (2023, January 10). How the U.S. Handles Its Waste. *The New York Times*. https://www.nytimes.com/2023/01/10/climate/us-recycling-waste.html

Preeti, S. (2023). Municipal Solid Waste Management: Challenges and Solutions. *Waste Management & Research*. https://doi.org/10.1177/0734242X231152556

Solid Waste Observation Public Account. (2022). China's Waste Segregation Progress Report. *WeChat Official Account*. https://mp.weixin.qq.com/s/-A4-YCn4bHKpSv9tH_fmAA

Technology Leader. (2020). China's Waste Management Technology Advancements. *Sohu News*. https://www.sohu.com/a/386410567_120085520

Wan, Junyi, Xinru Feng, Qixu Tang, et al. "Cost-Benefit Analysis of Harmless Disposal of Municipal Solid Waste: A Case Study of 25 Cities in China." *Resources and Industries* 21, no. 4 (2019): 81–89.

Weber Consulting. "Overview of the Waste Incineration Power Generation Industry in the United States: Includes Development History, Business Model, and Analysis of Leading." *Polaris Waste Power Grid*, 2020. Accessed December 2, 2023. https://mhuanbao.bjx.com.cn/mnews/20201202/1119449.shtml.

Yu, C., D. Jin, X. Hu, W. He, and G. Li. "An Overview of Management Status and Recycling Strategies for Plastic Packaging Waste in China." *Recycling*, 2023.

Chapter 2
Comparison of Policies Targeting the Reduction of Greenhouse Gas (GHG) Emissions from Food Waste in the US and China

2.1 Section Summary

Methane emissions, the second-largest contributor to greenhouse gasses after carbon dioxide, significantly impact global warming. According to the United Nations Environment Programme (UNEP) and the Climate & Clean Air Coalition (CCAC), reducing methane emissions could potentially avoid nearly 0.3 °C of global warming by the 2040s, offering critical time to implement more ambitious carbon reduction measures. Studies indicate that targeting methane emissions could provide even greater benefits in mitigating climate change than focusing solely on CO_2 reductions.

Recognizing their status as the top two methane emitters globally, both China and the US have prioritized methane emission reductions. This commitment is reflected in their bilateral dialogues, such as the April 2021 U.S.-China Joint Statement Addressing the Climate Crisis and other subsequent agreements. This section, analyzes methane emission trends from landfills in the two countries, examining current policies and challenges in emission reduction efforts.

2.1.1 *Overview of Global Greenhouse Gas Emissions*

Methane levels have risen since the 1850s, reaching 1866 parts per billion (ppb) in 2019. Current policies, depicted in models by the IPCC, fall short of meeting 2030 and 2050 targets, underscoring severe challenges.

H. Huang et al., *Waste Management for Global Sustainability*, CSR, Sustainability, Ethics & Governance, https://doi.org/10.1007/978-981-96-8305-5_2

2.1.2 Methane Emissions in the US and China

China and the US account for one-fourth of global methane emissions. Recent reports indicate 55 $TgCH_4$ from China and 28 $TgCH_4$ from the US. From 1990 to 2020, China saw an increase in methane emissions due to the energy and waste sectors. In contrast, the US emissions peaked before 2000 and have since declined, with a decrease of approximately 4.8 $TgCH_4$ during the same period.

2.1.3 Methane Emission Composition

China's emissions from waste have shown consistent growth, whereas US emissions from landfills have decreased significantly, nearly halving over thirty years. This demonstrates the effectiveness of US policies in reducing landfill emissions, setting an example for China and globally.

2.1.4 Additional Insights on Methane Emissions

Food waste, a major component of landfill methane emissions, decomposes anaerobically to release methane. In the US, food and plastic wastes are the primary sources of landfill methane. China's treatment of food waste remains low, with a notable portion still ending in landfills, highlighting the need for improved management practices.

2.1.5 Landfill Gas (LFG) Estimation and Utilization

Effective methane reduction strategies require accurate estimation and measurement of landfill gas (LFG). The first order degradation (FOD) model was widely used for analyzing the methane emission from landfills, while other monitoring measures such as interpretation of satellite remote sensing images and onsite monitoring. Both the U.S. and China established a well collection system of landfill gas, however, the utilizing rate (transforming methane into electricity or heat) still remains unclear due to the insufficient of statistics.

2.2 Trends in Greenhouse Gas Emissions from Food Waste and Solid Waste in China and the United States

Methane emissions are a critical focus in the effort to mitigate global warming, as they are the second-largest contributor to greenhouse gas (GHG) emissions after carbon dioxide. According to the United Nations Environment Programme (UNEP) and the Climate & Clean Air Coalition (CCAC), reducing methane emissions could prevent nearly 0.3 °C of global warming by the 2040s. This would provide additional time to implement more ambitious measures to reduce carbon emissions. Studies by Dreyfus et al. (2022) and Hope (2005) suggest that reducing methane emissions can more significantly decrease warming and offer greater marginal benefits than reducing CO_2 emissions.[1,2]

Both the Chinese and United States governments have recognized the importance of methane emission reductions, given that these countries are the largest and second-largest methane emitters globally. Their collaboration on this issue has become a vital part of their bilateral dialogue, as evidenced by recurring mentions in joint statements over the past three years. For instance, methane emission control was highlighted in the April 2021 U.S.-China Joint Statement Addressing the Climate Crisis, the November 2021 U.S.-China Joint Glasgow Declaration on Enhancing Climate Action in the 2020s, and the November 2023 Sunnylands Statement on Enhancing Cooperation to Address the Climate Crisis.

This report examined the trends in methane emissions in both China and the US, with a specific focus on emissions from landfills. It will analyze current policies and the challenges faced in implementing emission reduction strategies. By breaking down the analysis results, this report will identify opportunities for more effective emission reduction initiatives and potential areas for collaborative efforts between China and the US.

2.2.1 Overview of Global Greenhouse Gas Emissions from IPCC

According to the IPCC, methane emissions have been rising since the 1850s, reaching 1866 parts per billion (ppb) in 2019 (Fig. 2.1). Figure 2.2 illustrates methane (CH_4) emissions over time, measured in giga tonnes of CO_2 equivalent (Gt CO_2eq). The brown line shows historical emissions and projected emissions under policies implemented until the end of 2020 (grey), along with pathways consistent with various

[1] G. Dreyfus, B. Xu, D.T. Shindell, D. Zaelke, and V. Ramanathan, "Mitigating Climate Disruption in Time: A Self-Consistent Approach for Avoiding Both Near-Term and Long-Term Global Warming," *Proceedings of the National Academy of Sciences* 119, no. 22 (2022), https://doi.org/10.1073/pnas.2123536119.

[2] C. Hope, "The Climate Change Benefits of Reducing Methane Emissions," *Climatic Change* 68, no. 1 (2005): 21–39.

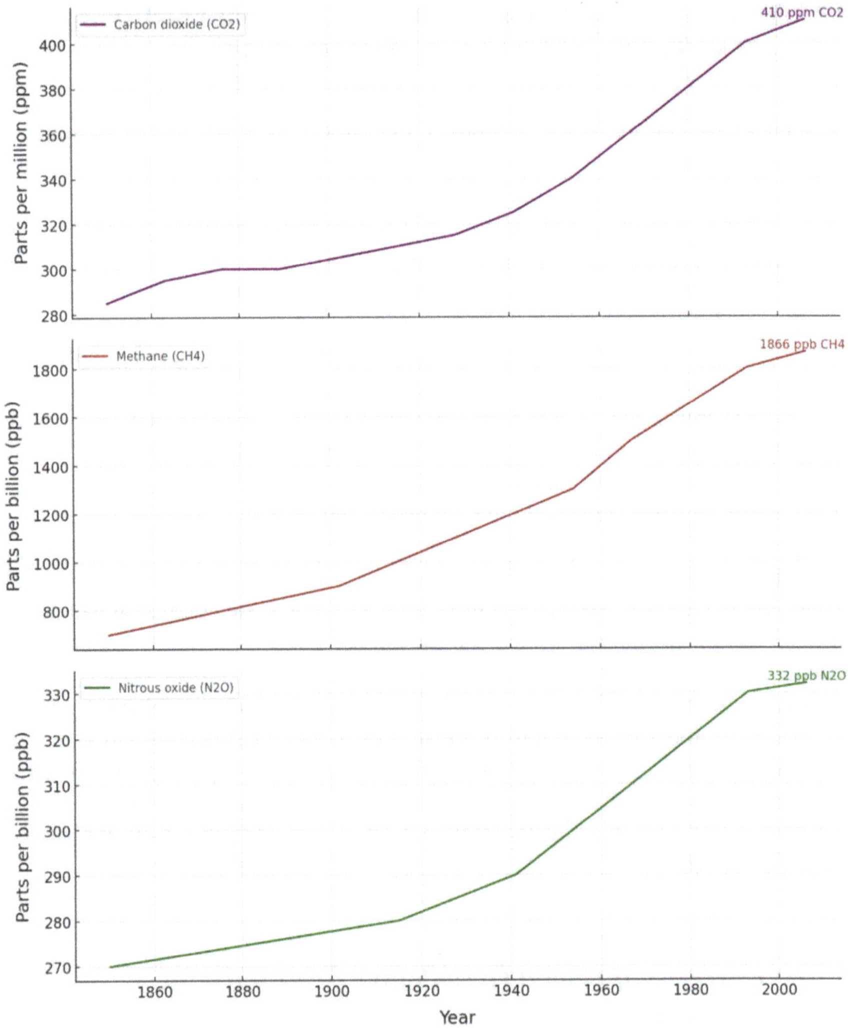

Fig. 2.1 GHG trend since 1850

temperature goals (blue, purple, and brown). Panel (a) (left) displays pathways that limit warming to 1.5 °C (>50%) with no or limited overshoot (C1), and Panel (b) (right) shows pathways that limit warming to 2 °C (>67%) (C3).[3] The data indicates that the current policies are insufficient to meet the 2030 and 2050 targets, highlighting the severe challenges we face.

[3] IPCC, *Climate Change 2023 Synthesis Report*, 2023.

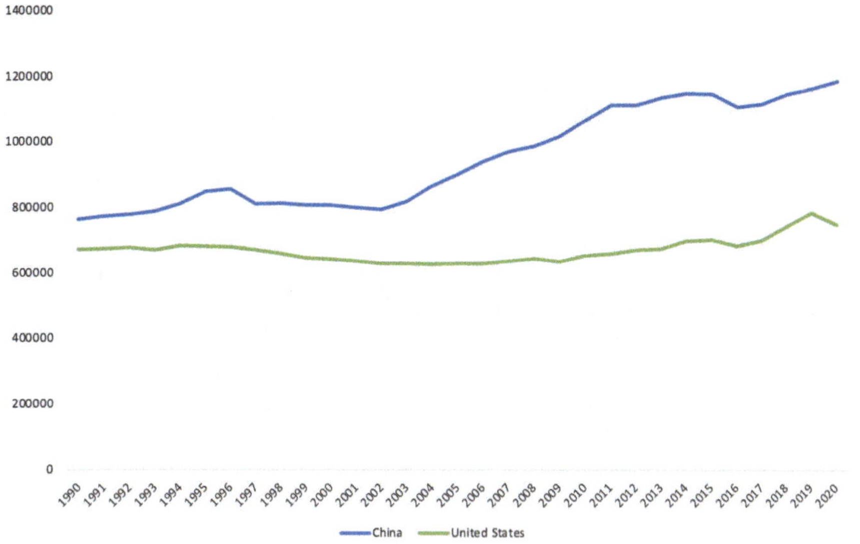

Fig. 2.2 Overview of Methane Emissions in U.S. and China (*Source* Yu et al., 2022)

2.2.2 Overview of Methane Emissions in U.S. and China

To effectively take action in reducing methane emissions, it is essential to display the current status in the US and China, including historical data and future estimates of overall emissions as well as breakdowns from all sources. According to GMI (2022), methane emissions from China and the US account for one-fourth of global emissions. In the most recent official methane reports, China and the US reported total methane emissions of 55 $TgCH_4$ and 28 $TgCH_4$, respectively.[4,5] This highlights their significant role in driving positive global changes in methane emissions.

Figure 2.2 illustrates the national methane emissions estimated by several models applied to China and the US. For China, inventories with time-series data show a consistent long-term trend of increasing total methane emissions from 1990 to 2020, mainly due to the energy and waste sectors, despite slight differences in the estimated results between models. In contrast, the US has shown a decrease in total methane emissions by approximately 4.8 $TgCH_4$ from 1990 to 2020. Bottom-up inventories generally agree on the overall trend, showing emissions declining from 1994–2005, increasing slightly between 2005 and 2008, and then decreasing through 2016, before

[4] *China NCCC, The People's Republic of China Second Biennial Update Report on Climate Change 2018*, https://unfccc.int/sites/default/files/resource/China%202BUR_English.pdf.

[5] Environmental Protection Agency, "Coalbed Methane Outreach Program (CMOP)," 2022, https://www.epa.gov/cmop.

a slight increase in the latest data. Emissions in the US peaked before 2000 and have been slowly declining since.[6]

At the provincial level, this report refers to China's methane emission map estimated by the First-order Decay (FOD) model from the Intergovernmental Panel on Climate Change (IPCC) and the US methane emission map estimated by the Landfill Gas Emission Model (LandGEM) from the United States Environmental Protection Agency.[7,8] Despite statistical discrepancies due to period and models, comparisons are still significant. Both countries have major emissions concentrated in their eastern regions, where around 96% and 80% of the population live in China and the US, respectively. When comparing emission levels, the most intense emission areas in eastern China are higher than those in eastern US, with 150,000 metric tons (1 Gg = 1000 metric tons) compared to 33,000 metric tons. This ratio is similar to the population density ratio in China and the US, which is 150 to 36 people per square kilometer.[9,10] (Fig. 2.3).

2.2.3 Composition of National Methane Emissions in the U.S. And China

Regarding the composition of national methane emissions, many models estimate emissions from solid waste, particularly food waste. Similar to the overall trend, China's emissions from waste show that there is consistent growth, while US emissions from landfills exhibit a decreasing trend with a steeper decline. This indicates that policies aimed at reducing methane emissions from landfills have been effective. The nearly 50% reduction in methane emissions from US landfills over thirty years demonstrates the feasibility and effectiveness of these policies, bolstering confidence in the ability to control methane emissions to reasonable levels from landfills in both the US and China. These successful examples can serve as a model for global methane emission control efforts (Figs. 2.4 and 2.5).

According to the composition of national methane emissions from both countries, many models estimate emissions from solid waste, mainly food waste. Similar to the overall trend of methane emissions, emissions from waste in China show constant

---

[6] Yu, Shao, Jan Behrendt, Min Zhu, Xinyi Cheng, Weichen Li, Bin Liu, et al. "Roadmap for US-China Methane Collaboration: Methane Emissions, Mitigation Potential, and Policies Summary for Policymakers." 2022.

[7] S. Qu, D. Guan, Z. Ma, and X. Yi, "A Study on the Optimal Path of Methane Emissions Reductions in a Municipal Solid Waste Landfill Treatment Based on the IPCC-SD Model," *Journal of Cleaner Production* 222 (2019): 252–266.

[8] Environmental Protection Agency, "Advancements in U.S. Recycling and Waste Management," 2021, https://www.epa.gov/.

[9] World Bank, "CO2 Emissions (Metric Tons per Capita)," https://data.worldbank.org/indicator/EN.ATM.CO2E.PC.

[10] World Bank, "Methane Emissions (Kt of CO2 Equivalent)—China, United States," accessed August 7, 2024, https://data.worldbank.org/indicator/EN.ATM.METH.KT.CE?locations=CN-US.

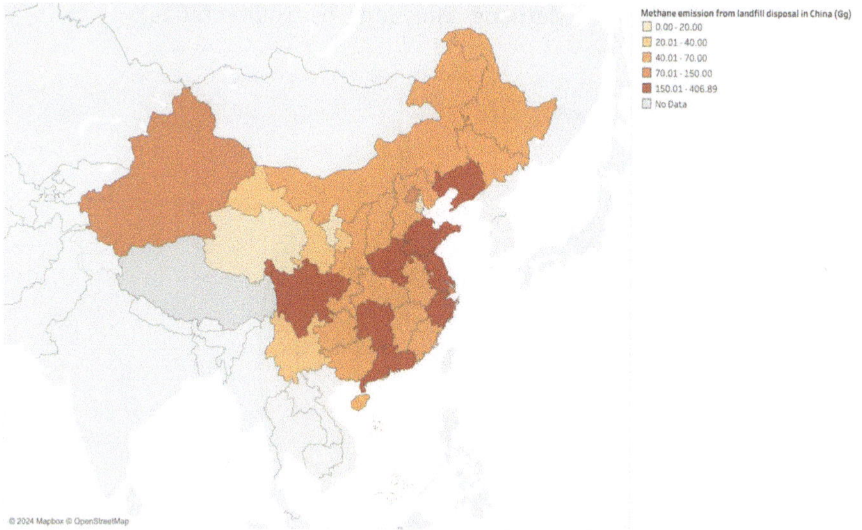

Fig. 2.3 Comparison of Methane Emissions from Landfill Disposal in China at Provincial Level (*Source* [Qu et al., 2019], [Chinese EPA 2022])

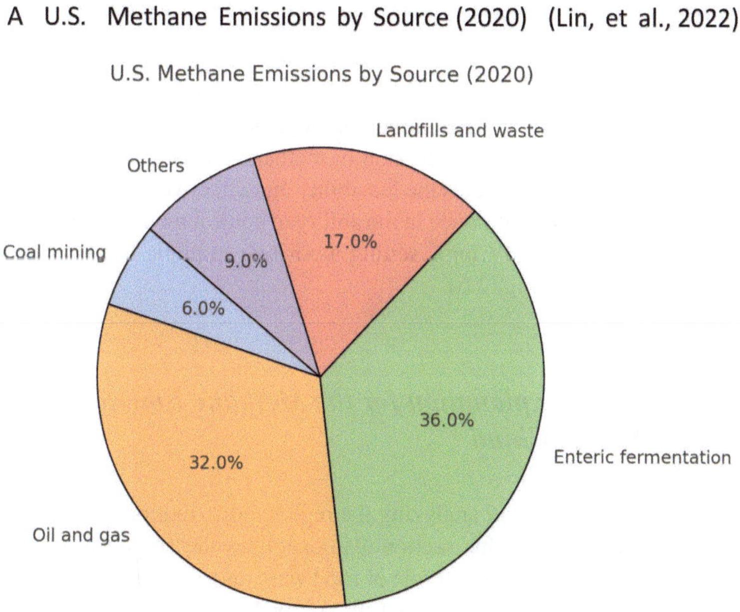

Fig. 2.4 U.S. Methane Emissions by Source (2020) (Lin et al., 2022)

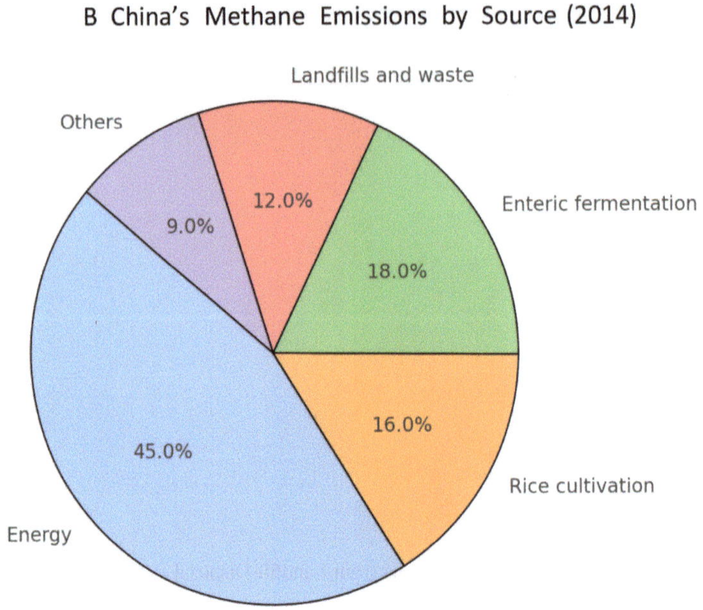

Fig. 2.5 China's Methane Emissions by Source (2014) (*Source* Lin et al., 2022)

growth, while US emissions from landfills show a decreasing trend with a steeper decline. This indicates that policies targeting methane reduction from landfills have been effective. The nearly 50% reduction in methane emissions from US landfills over thirty years also demonstrates the feasibility and effectiveness of these policies. This success strengthens confidence in the ability to control methane emissions from landfills in both the US and China, setting a positive example for global methane emission control efforts (Fig. 2.6).

2.2.4 Additional Explanation for the Methane Emissions in U.S. And China

In addition to quantifying and analyzing the regional distribution of methane emissions in China and the US, this section also examines the composition of landfill waste and highlights the significant role of food waste as a source of landfill methane emissions. Food waste, which is primarily composed of organic material, undergoes biological degradation that consumes interstitial oxygen, making the waste pile anaerobic. Under suitable redox conditions, methanogenesis occurs, releasing methane as a waste gas from landfill sites.

In the US, as shown in the figure, food waste, paper and paperboard are the top two sources of methane emission from landfills. Paper and paperboard waste has a

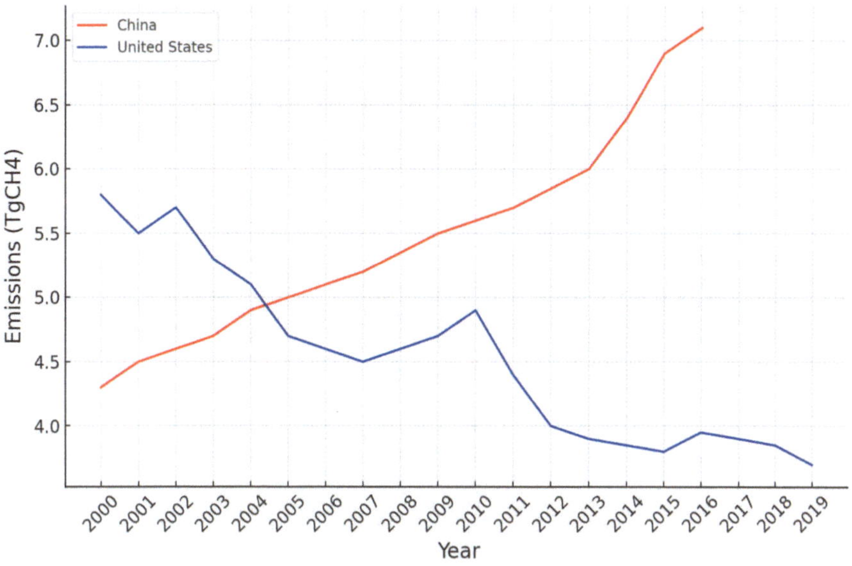

Fig. 2.6 Emissions Estimation from Solid Waste Based on Composition (*Source* Yu et al., 2022)

high concentration of degradable organic carbon, which can result a large methane emission from landfills. Although there is no statistical data on landfill composition in China, the treatment data of food waste can be used to infer its significant presence in Chinese landfills. According to Dou (2015), the recovery rate of food waste in China was only 1–2.1% in 2012.[11] By 2020, only 10% of food waste was treated by anaerobic digestion, while 49% and 41% were sent to incineration and landfilling, respectively, after being mixed with municipal solid waste.[12] This highlights the importance of addressing food waste in China's efforts to reduce landfill methane emissions (Figs. 2.7 and 2.8).

From the perspective of municipal solid waste (MSW), half of the MSW goes to landfills, producing methane emissions, the third largest source of anthropogenic methane. Food waste (FW) and paper waste are the two most significant sources of methane in MSW due to their organic components as shown in Fig. 2.12. In terms of public health, improper management of landfill sites, for example the onsite burning of plastics can lead to the leaching of toxic chemicals, polluting the surrounding environment, in addition to the carbon emission from fossil carbon combusting (Narevski et al., 2021). Additionally, microplastics have been detected in landfill leachate and

[11] X. Dou, "Food Waste Generation and Its Recycling Recovery: China's Governance Mode and Its Assessment," *Fresenius Environmental Bulletin* 24, no. 4A (2015): 1474–82.

[12] M. Shen, W. Huang, M. Chen, B. Song, G. Zeng, and Y. Zhang, "(Micro)Plastic Crisis: Un-Ignorable Contribution to Global Greenhouse Gas Emissions and Climate Change," *Journal of Cleaner Production* 254 (May 2020): 120138, https://doi.org/10.1016/j.jclepro.2020.120138.

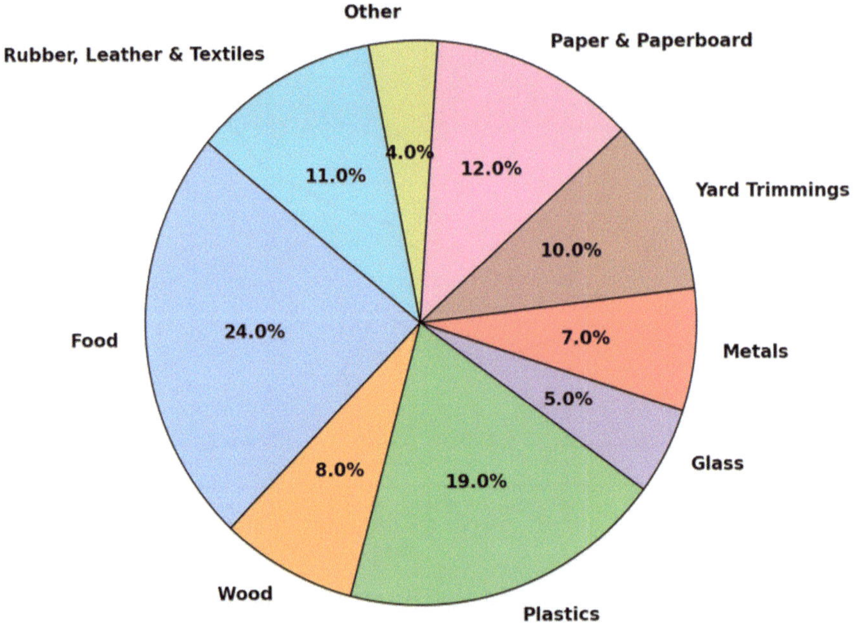

Fig. 2.7 Components of Landfills in the US (*Source* EPA 2018)

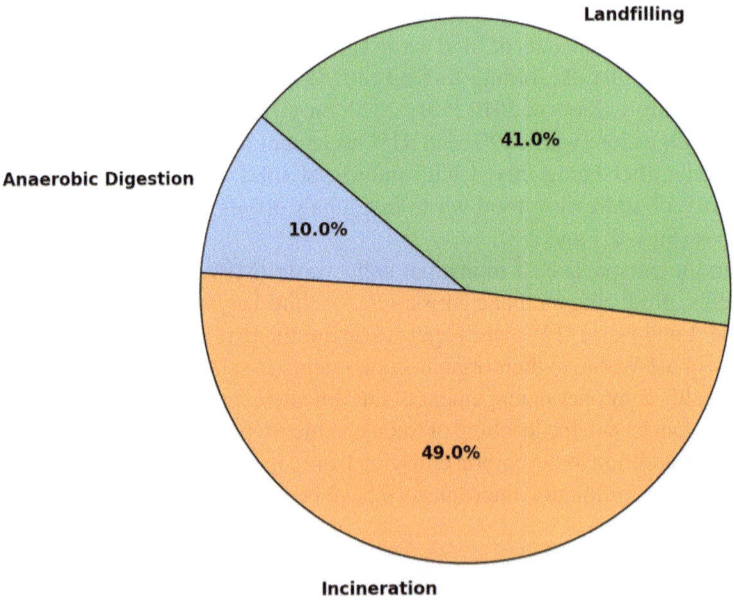

Fig. 2.8 Food Waste Treatment in China (*Source* Liu et al., 2020; 2022; Dou, 2015)

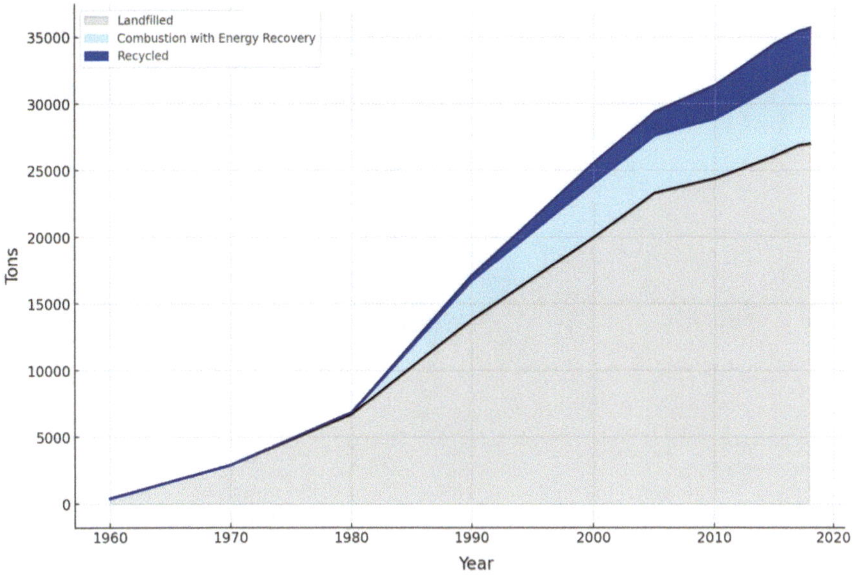

Fig. 2.9 Plastics Waste Management from 1960 to 2018 (*Source* Heller et al., 2020)

surrounding soil environment, throwing threat to human health of the residential areas[13,14]

In the United States, more than three-quarters of the plastic reaching the end of its life went to landfills, and less than 8% was recycled in 2017.[15] The trend of plastic waste in the US can be seen in the figure. In China, 52% of the MSW is disposed of in landfills, with rubber and plastics accounting for 9.9% ~ 19.1% of the MSW.[16] Therefore, to address MSW issues, there should be a stronger emphasis on recycling food and plastic waste instead of simply dumping them in landfills, which exacerbates environmental problems (Figs. 2.9 and 2.10).

By analyzing the three main sources of methane emissions, this paper identifies landfill methane emissions as a critical target for reduction through strengthened policymaking and implementation for several reasons. Unlike emissions from the oil

---

[13] P. He, L. Chen, L. Shao, H. Zhang, and F. Lü, "Municipal Solid Waste (MSW) Landfill: A Source of Microplastics? Evidence of Microplastics in Landfill Leachate," *Water Research* 159 (2019): 38–45.

[14] J. Sun, Z.R. Zhu, W.H. Li, X.F. Yan, L.K. Wang, L. Zhang, J.B. Jin, X.H. Dai, B.J. Ni, "Revisiting Microplastics in Landfill Leachate: Unnoticed Tiny Microplastics and Their Fate in Treatment Works," *Water Research* 190 (2021): 116784.

[15] M.C. Heller, M.H. Mazor, and G.A. Keoleian, "Plastics in the US: Toward a Material Flow Characterization of Production, Markets, and End of Life," *Environmental Research Letters* 15 (2020): 094034.

[16] Y. Ding, J.-W. Zhao, J. Liu, et al., "A Review of China's Municipal Solid Waste (MSW) and Comparison with International Regions: Management and Technologies in Treatment and Resource Utilization," *Journal of Cleaner Production* 293 (2021): 126144.

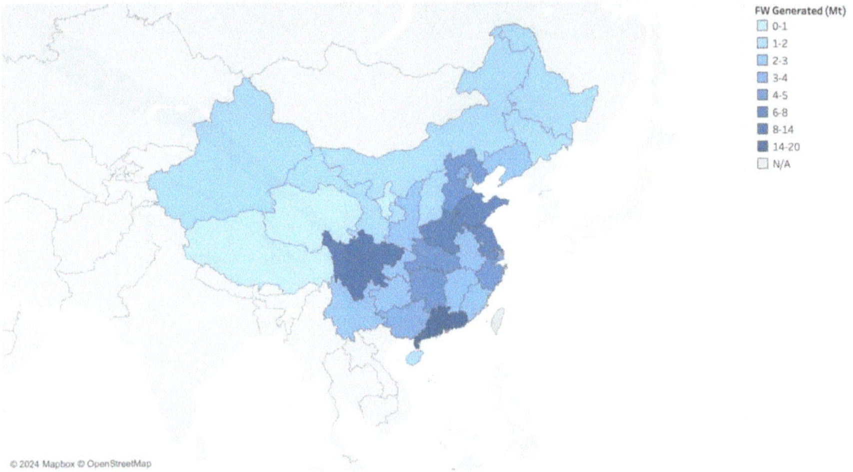

Fig. 2.10 Provincial Distribution of Food waste (FW) Generation in China (*Source* NBSC 2019)[17]

and gas industry, the cost of reducing emissions from landfills is lower due to the predictable location of emissions sites. A relatively fixed set of techniques can be used to collect methane from landfills. In contrast, methane emissions from oil and gas sites arise from various sources, including leaks from pipelines and equipment, venting, and flaring of gas, requiring a variety of technologies to efficiently collect the methane. Compared to livestock emissions, reducing methane from landfills is more efficient because landfill sites are centralized and static, unlike the discrete, large-scale, and dynamic nature of livestock emissions. Additionally, technologies for mitigating livestock methane emissions involve complex and costly processes such as fermentation, genetic selection, and management practices to improve feed efficiency.

2.3 Landfill Gas (LFG) Estimation, Measurement and Utilization in China and U.S.

2.3.1 Current Model and Technology for Landfill Emission Estimation and Measurement

In dealing with greenhouse gasses from current landfills, accurate data on gas generation, emissions, and recovery are critical for understanding the efficiency of policies. Landfill gas (LFG) data are estimated based on past waste disposal histories and

[17] The amount of Food waste (FW) is obtained by the author's calculation, while GDP and urban population are mainly from the China Statistic Yearbook.

Table 2.1 MSW Default Values per Region (IPCC)

Region	MSW generation Rate (tonnes/cap/yr)	Fraction of MSW open dumped	Fraction of MSW disposed to landfills	Fraction of MSW incinerated	Fraction of MSW composted	Fraction of other MSW management, unspecified
Asia						
Eastern Asia	0.48	0.00	0.23	0.24	0.00	0.52
Central Asia	0.34					
South-Eastern Asia	0.46					
Southern Asia	0.50					
Western Asia	0.69	0.11	0.68	0.08	0.01	0.12
America						
Caribbean	0.78	0.03	0.78	0.00	0.01	0.18
Central America	0.58	0.13	0.62	0.00	0.00	0.25
South America	0.43	0.43	0.40	0.00	0.00	0.18
Northern America	0.96	0.00	0.22	0.26	0.13	0.38

estimates of collection system efficiency.[18] Specifically, the estimated emissions can be a combination of methane generation, consumption (methane oxidation), and transportation. Methane generation and consumption determine the general production of methane emissions from landfills, which depend on measurements at aerial sites. Transportation is accounted for by the efficiency of the system utilizing the generated methane, which subtracts from the total emissions. The most well-known landfill methane emission models are the quantitative IPCC models (Tier 1, Tier 2, and Tier 3) and the Landfill Gas Emission Model (LandGEM) from USEPA.

IPCC has developed a Tier 1 basic model to calculate CH_4 emissions based on default emission factors and national annual municipal solid waste disposal quantities. This model is suitable for countries that lack regional geographical climate data (e.g., temperature and rainfall) on MSW, which is a critical factor in determining methane emissions from landfills. The MSW default values for the US and China were shown in the following Table 2.1.

The Tier 2 method is a first-order decay (FOD) method, which not only depends on MSW decomposition emission rates but also considers the impact of geographical climate conditions (e.g., rainfall), as climate and soil conditions in different areas can significantly influence methane release rates from bio-methanogenesis. The FOD method requires good quality country-specific activity data (including waste generation for bulk waste or by waste component and the fraction of waste disposed to solid

[18] *Landfill Methane Outreach Program (LMOP), LFG Energy Project Development Handbook*, 2015, paged in sections, available at: https://www3.epa.gov/lmop/documents/pdfs/pdf_full.pdf.

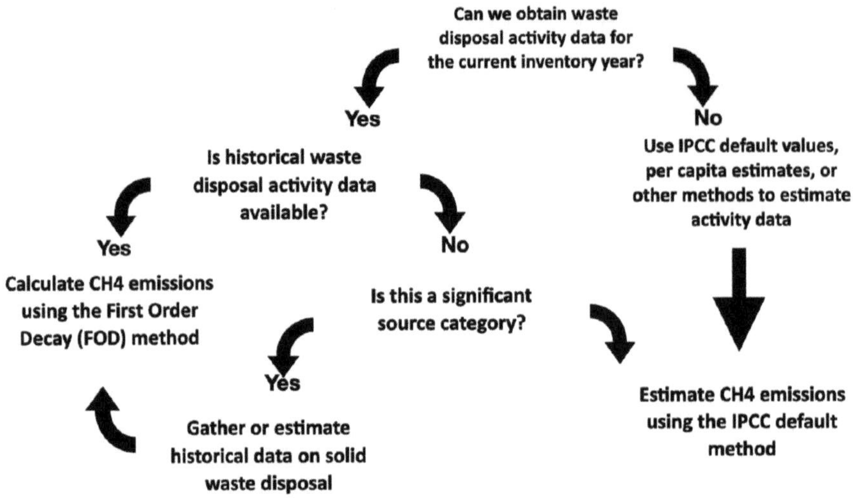

Fig. 2.11 Decision Tree for CH4 Emissions from Solid Waste Disposal Site (*Source* Galbally 2000)

waste disposal sites, or SWDS) on current and historical waste disposal at SWDSs. In national inventories, it is usually necessary to include data for three to five half-lives to achieve an acceptably accurate result. Changes in waste management practices (e.g., landfill covering/capping, leachate drainage improvement, compacting, and prohibition of hazardous waste disposal with MSW) should also be considered when compiling historical data.[19] This method is generally used for both the US and China. For example, the LandGEM from USEPA is based on FOD methods (Fig. 2.11).

LandGEM is a model that relies on FOD methods to calculate CH_4 and non-methane organic compound emission rates from MSW landfills. The LandGEM model is very specific due to its reliance on geographical climate conditions (e.g., rainfall) and waste disposal data. If the MSW generation data is overestimated, the landfill methane emission results will be significantly overestimated.[20]

For countries with very good data sets, “Tier 3” methods are based on FOD methods but emphasize more sophisticated data, including emission factors applied to specific landfills or actual data on CH_4 emissions from sites.[21] The Tier 3 method is the most demanding but has become increasingly necessary as it provides the

[19] J. Penman, D. Kruger, I. Galbally, T. Hiraishi, B. Nyenzi, S. Emmanul, L. Buendia, R. Hoppaus, T. Martinsen, J. Meijer, K. Miwa, and K. Tanabe, eds., *Good Practice Guidance and Uncertainty Management in National Greenhouse Gas Inventories* (Japan: Institute for Global Environmental Strategies, 2000), ISBN 4-88788-000-6, https://www.ipcc.ch/publication/good-practice-guidance-and-uncertainty-management-in-national-greenhouse-gas-inventories/.

[20] J.T. Powell, T.G. Townsend, and J.B. Zimmerman, “Estimates of Solid Waste Disposal Rates and Reduction Targets for Landfill Gas Emissions,” *Nature Climate Change* (2015), https://doi.org/10.1038/NCLIMATE2804.

[21] X. Chai, D.J. Tonjes, and D. Mahajan, “Methane Emissions as Energy Reservoir: Context, Scope, Causes, and Mitigation Strategies,” *Progress in Energy and Combustion Science* 56 (2016): 33–70.

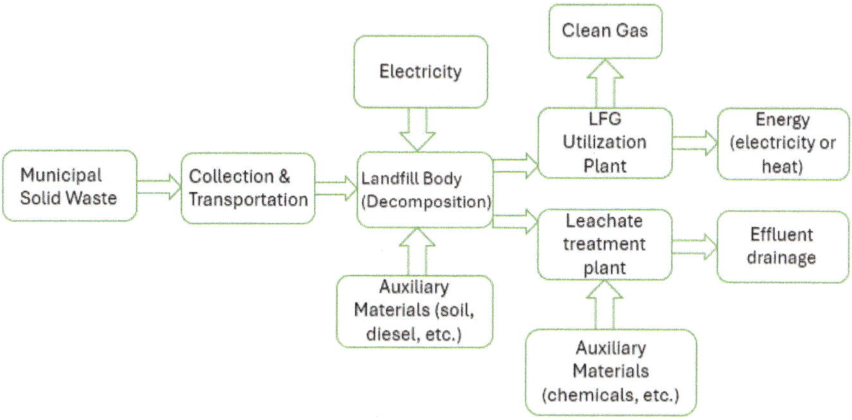

Fig. 2.12 MSW Landfilling LFGTE Technology (*Source* [Yang et al. 2013])

most accurate emission estimation data. This method requires good quality country-specific activity data and the use of either the FOD method with (1) nationally developed key parameters or (2) measurement-derived country-specific parameters. Common parameters for models can be found in the Table, and an example of default values for the parameter DOC_f set by IPCC can be viewed in the following Tables 2.2 and 2.3.

When applying this method, factors such as site precipitation, preferential flow paths within the waste mass, the distribution of methanotrophs in cover soils, and underlying waste quality and history all affect measurements at a particular landfill

Table 2.2 Key Parameters for FOD model setting (Page 60)

Abbreviation	Parameter	Meaning
DOC	Degradable organic carbon	Organic carbon in waste accessible to biochemical decomposition
DOCF	Fraction of degradable organic carbon that decomposes	Fraction of carbon released from SWDS under anaerobic conditions
MCF	CH_4 correction factor	Adjusts CH_4 production from unmanaged SWDS
F	Fraction of CH_4 in landfill gas	Default 0.5, Adjust 0.4–0.6 based on region
OX	Oxidation factor	Amount of CH_4 oxidized in SWDS soil or cover material
T1/2	Half-life value	Time for DOCm in waste to decay to half its initial mass
R	Methane Recovery	CH_4 recovered and combusted from SWDS
DT	Delay Time	Time before CH_4 production begins after waste deposition

Table 2.3 Fraction of Degradable Organic Carbon Which Decomposes (DOCf) for different waste types (page 60)

Type of waste	Recommended default DOCf values	Remark
Less decomposable wastes e.g. wood, engineered wood products, tree branches (wood)	0.1	An average value of 0.088 was derived from DOCf values for engineered wood products, sawn woods, tree branches reported in 3 references[1] to[3]
Moderately decomposable wastes e.g. paper, textile, nappies	0.5	An average value of 0.523 was derived from DOCf values for paper products, textile, and nappies reported in 4 references[4]to[7]
Highly decomposable wastes, e.g. food wastes, grasses (garden and park waste excluding tree branches)	0.7	An average value of 0.706 was derived from DOCf values for food wastes and grasses reported in 3 references [4]to[6]
Bulk waste*	0.5	

[1]Wang et al. (2011); [2] Wang and Barlaz (2016); [3] Ximenes et al. (2018); [4] Eleazer et al. (1997); [5] Bayard et al. (2017); [6] Jeong (2016); [7] Wang et al. (2015)
* It is used when the fraction of less, moderately and highly decomposable wastes in MSW are not known

site. Barometric pressure has also been identified as a key environmental control on measurements of release rates. The measurement techniques used also cause different results. Despite the few studies and lack of data for these ingrained factors, there are many opportunities to improve the accuracy of landfill methane emission estimations, particularly by applying measurement techniques more extensively than mere estimation.

2.3.2 *Landfill Gas Utilization*

Consistent with the analysis in estimating and measuring landfill gas, this report introduces landfill gas utilization systems, known as Landfill Gas to Energy (LFGTE) systems. Traditionally, landfill gas has escaped into the atmosphere through the slow decomposition of waste or the flaring of waste to expedite the process, contributing significantly to greenhouse gas emissions and local smog. LFGTE projects capture

Table 2.4 Estimated Economic Benefits from LFGTE Project (page 63)

Estimated regional (State-wide) economic benefits	Typical 3-MW Engine Project	Typical 1000 scfm Direct-use Project (5-mile pipeline)	Typical 2800 scfm RNG Project (2-mile pipeline)
Direct effects			
Project expenditures for the purchase of generators, piping, and gas compression, treatment skid and auxiliary equipment	\$3.74 million	\$2.68 million	\$5.37 million
Jobs created	9.6	14.6	18.5
Indirect effects			
Economic output, resulting from ripple effects	\$8.35 to \$9.54 million	\$5.41 to \$6.40 million	\$11.93 to \$13.50 million
Jobs created, including economic ripple effects	34.5–44.6	32.4–40.0	53.2–67.7

methane gas for electricity and heat, turning a harmful source of waste into a beneficial source of renewable energy.[22] The figure shows the overall process of LFGTE (Fig. 2.12).

There are several benefits associated with this system. First, methane gas accumulating underground poses direct and indirect risks to nearby communities. Methane is flammable and can explode under high pressure in confined spaces. Continued accumulation of untreated landfill gas may cause explosions, endangering human surroundings. Additionally, leaked methane can elevate regional methane levels in the soil, posing health hazards through contaminated groundwater and food grown in affected areas. Thus, reducing methane levels in landfills can benefit neighboring communities (Table 2.4).

Second, as global warming is a critical issue today, any technique that reduces GHG emissions is beneficial. Installing LFGTE systems in landfills collects methane rather than releasing it, contributing to the goal of reducing global methane emissions, especially in the US and China, the two largest emitters of methane. Moreover, landfill energy generation systems can generate substantial economic benefits. The following table shows the economic benefits of the USEPA Landfill Gas Energy Project Construction (Figs. 2.13).

According to the latest US EPA data, as of March 2024, there are 2637 landfill sites and 756 Landfill Gas Energy Projects in the US.[23] These 756 projects generate

[22] Yang, Ning, Hong Zhang, Lin Mei Shao, Feng Lü, and Peng Ji He. "Greenhouse Gas Emissions During MSW Landfilling in China: Influence of Waste Characteristics and LFG Treatment Measures." *Journal of Environmental Management* 129 (2013): 510–521.

[23] U.S. Environmental Protection Agency, "Landfill Gas Energy Project Data," accessed August 7, 2024, https://www.epa.gov/lmop/landfill-gas-energy-project-data.

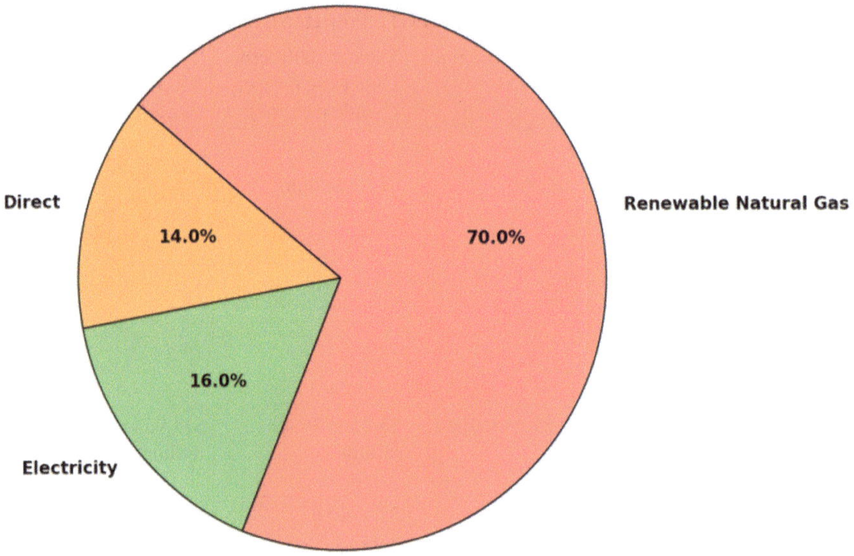

Fig. 2.13 US Landfill Gas Energy Projects Distribution (*Source EPA Landfill Gas Energy Projects Database 2024)*

electricity, fire kilns, upgrade LFG into pipeline-quality gas, for further use in greenhouses and buildings for heating, and provide steam for industrial processes. In comparison, in 2020, China constructed 510 LFGTE plants with an annual production capacity of 193 million tons.[24]

2.4 Overview of Food Waste Management Policies and Regulations in China and the United States

2.4.1 Overview of China's Food Waste Management Policies and Regulations

2.4.1.1 Concepts Related to Food and Organic Waste

In various policies or status and regulations, differences in regulatory objectives and subjects result in variations in the terminology and conceptual frameworks concerning regulations on organic waste. Although these policies all contain provisions related to the regulation of organic waste, they often adopt naming conventions based on existing legal concepts or the entities being regulated. For example, the "Law

[24] N. J. Themelis and W. Ma, "Waste to Energy (WTE) in China: From Latecomer to Front Runner," *Waste Disposal & Sustainable Energy* 3 (2021): 267–274.

on the Prevention and Control of Environment Pollution Caused by Solid Wastes," which serves as a comprehensive legal framework for waste management, does not specify standards for waste classification but assigns responsibility for establishing municipal waste classification management systems to local governments at or above the county level. Consequently, subordinate regulations and specialized legal enactments concerning organic waste may not consistently align with expressions found in other legal instruments.

For instance, the "*Beijing Regulation on the Management of Municipal Waste*" and the "*Shanghai Regulation on the Management of Municipal Waste*" exemplify this discrepancy. While Beijing's regulatory framework for managing organic waste predominantly centers on the concept of kitchen waste (food waste from restaurant), Shanghai's municipal ordinances employ the term "wet waste"(food waste from household and wet market) as a blanket designation for the category organic waste. Similarly, specialized legislation such as the "*Anti-Food Waste Law*" of China primarily aimed at curbing food wastage falls within the realm of waste management discussed in this discourse. However, owing to its regulatory focus on food, a category not strictly confined within the realm of waste, the definition of food therein explicitly adopts the parameters set forth in the "*Food Safety Law*" ("food for human consumption or drinking").

However, despite the scenario where the use of identical terminology across divergent regulatory contexts, the semantic scope of such terms remains inconsistent. For instance, the recurring concepts of "restaurant food waste", "household food waste" and "food waste from wet market" In reference to the 2012 industry standard document "*Technical Specifications for the Treatment of Kitchen Waste*" issued by the Ministry of Housing and Urban–Rural Development, " restaurant food waste" denotes residual food from food service providers or byproducts generated during food processing, while " household food waste " primarily refers to organic waste originating from household activities.[25] Moreover, food waste serves as an umbrella term encompassing both categories. However, interpretations within regulatory frameworks may not rigidly adhere to these definitions. In essence, "kitchen waste" predominantly features in legal documentation as a colloquialism denoting organic waste within the municipal waste category. Both the "Prevention and Control of Solid Waste Pollution Law" and the "Anti-Food Waste Law" utilize "kitchen waste" as a general reference to organic waste. Conversely, local regulations, such as the "Regulations on the Management of Kitchen Waste in Sanya City," "Regulations on the Management of Kitchen Waste in Suihua City," and "Regulations on the Management of Kitchen Waste in Huai'an City," tailored to the governance of food waste, frequently incorporate stipulations delineating the subject matter to exclude organic waste originating from non-commercial activities of residents.

[25] National Development and Reform Commission, Ministry of Housing and Urban-Rural Development. "13th Five-Year Plan for the Development of Urban Living Waste Sorting and Treatment Facilities." December 2016. Accessed March 25, 2024. https://www.ndrc.gov.cn/resource/W020190905497906455466.pdf.

At the legal level, there are no exhaustive requirements for the landfilling process, with regulations governing organic waste generated post-landfilling being subject to the different harm objects under the "Air Pollution Prevention and Control Law," "Water Pollution Prevention and Control Law," and "Soil Pollution Prevention and Control Law." However, the issuance of the "Methane Emission Control Action Plan" by the Ministry of Ecology and Environment and other 11 departments primarily aims at controlling methane, a greenhouse gas, in landfilling processes. Besides reiterating the "reduction and resource utilization" requirements for domestic waste treatment, the plan also calls for the advancement of kitchen waste treatment facilities and landfill gas recovery and utilization levels. Furthermore, specific enforcement regulations for landfilling activities are guided by the "Pollution Control Standards for Domestic Waste Landfills (2008)," stipulating requirements for methane gas management, including the installation of gas drainage systems at landfills, and the emitted methane gas should meet the requirement of methane volume fraction not exceeding 5% after utilization or incineration.[26]

It is evident that the current regulatory framework for organic waste management primarily exists as components of laws related to food security, anti-food waste, or waste management, rather than as standalone law. At the enforcement level, regulations adopt a supervisory approach primarily targeting food processing and catering service entities at the generation and collection ends. This approach is due to the concentrated nature of waste generation and management demands compared to non-production activities of individual households. Additionally, constrained by limited administrative resources, there is a necessity to allocate resources to the most critical areas to maximize utility.[27] Consequently, compared to the comprehensive supervision imposed on non-profit individual units, regulatory supervision over commercial food processing and catering service entities is deemed more preferable in terms of priority and utility. In the backend "harmless" disposal, standards promulgated by responsible departments serve as the primary basis, supporting administrative management departments in their regulatory enforcement efforts in activities such as organic waste composting, landfilling, and incineration.

2.4.1.2 Regulation and Policy

Given the context of "*Law on the Prevention and Control of Environment Pollution Caused by Solid Wastes*" and related policy norms, the general requirements of "reduction, resource utilization, and harmlessness" proposed for waste management to not only focus on the waste treatment activities themselves but also encompass governance activities throughout the entire lifecycle of waste, including source

[26] Ministry of Ecology and Environment, "Standard for Pollution Control on the Landfill Site of Municipal Solid Waste," July 1, 2008, https://english.mee.gov.cn/Resources/standards/Solid_Waste/SW_control/200907/W020080709425609446011.pdf.

[27] B. Margaret Popoola, "Biodegradable Waste," in *IntechOpen* (2023), https://doi.org/10.5772/intechopen.107910.

control, circulation management, and end-of-life treatment. Therefore, this article comprehensively examines relevant norms and policies related to organic waste across the production, circulation, and treatment stages.[28]

Firstly, in the production and circulation stages, there are two main areas of work for reducing organic waste at the source: grain conservation and anti-food waste in food processing and catering production. Grain conservation involves initiatives outlined in the "Action Plan for Grain Conservation" issued by the General Office of the CPC Central Committee and the General Office of the State Council, which aims to establish systems, standards, and monitoring systems for reducing grain loss and waste by 2025.[29] Additionally, the "Grain Security Guarantee Law," enacted in 2023, requires measures to improve grain utilization and reduce unnecessary grain waste throughout production, transportation, storage, processing, and consumption.[30] Similarly, measures have been implemented to combat food waste in catering and food processing industries. For instance, in March 2014, the General Office of the CPC Central Committee and the General Office of the State Council issued the "Opinions on Strengthening Thrift and Opposing Food Waste," which outlined various measures to combat food waste in public dining and advocated for thrift in unit canteens. Furthermore, in April 2021, the "Anti-Food Waste Law" was promulgated, inheriting the content of previous documents and explicitly addressing the reduction of unnecessary food waste at the source.[31]

2.4.2 Overview of China's Organic Waste Management Policies and Regulations

2.4.2.1 Law and Policy

The United States has scarcely any federal status regarding organic waste management, as the vast majority of legislation and enforcement concerning organic waste management are delegated to the states and local authorities. Consequently, regulations pertaining to organic waste are more numerous in absolute terms but are relatively scattered, with significant variations in legislative content and a lack of high levels of systematization among localities. On the one hand, this is attributed to the early initiation of relevant legislative efforts. On the other hand, food waste

[28] Ministry of Ecology and Environment, "Standard for Pollution Control on the Landfill Site of Municipal Solid Waste," July 1, 2008, https://english.mee.gov.cn/Resources/standards/Solid_Waste/SW_control/200907/W020080709425609446011.pdf.

[29] General Office of the CPC Central Committee and the State Council, "Action Plan for Grain Conservation," https://english.mee.gov.cn/Resources/standards/Solid_Waste/SW_control/200907/W020080709425609446011.pdf.

[30] National People's Congress, "Grain Security Guarantee Law," 2023, https://english.mee.gov.cn/Resources/standards/Solid_Waste/SW_control/200907/W020080709425609446011.pdf.

[31] National People's Congress, "Anti-Food Waste Law," April 2021, https://english.mee.gov.cn/Resources/standards/Solid_Waste/SW_control/200907/W020080709425609446011.pdf.

is a prominent issue in the United States. The legislative efforts on organic waste focus heavily on addressing the issue of food waste. Adam Chandler highlighted in his 2016 article "Why Americans Lead the World in Food Waste" that Americans lead in food waste globally due to easy access to cheap calories combined with pickiness in food choices.[32] Regardless of one's agreement with Chandler's assertions, it cannot be denied that food waste in the United States has reached alarming levels. An article in The Guardian in 2016 cited research indicating that almost half of food products are wasted, with some interviewed farmers stating that nearly a quarter of agricultural products are abandoned in fields or used as livestock feed.[33] Therefore, legal measures to curb food waste and promote its recycling have been focal points in legislative activities.

With reference to the 2023 edition of the *Wasted Food Scale* published by the United States Environmental Protection Agency (EPA), policies and regulations concerning this matter can be categorized into six hierarchical levels, ranging from waste reduction at the source to final disposal methods such as landfilling, incineration, and simple disposal as most preferred to least preferred.[34] Each level of measures builds upon the previous one, with an emphasis on implementing the highest level of measures possible before considering lower-level ones. In comparison to systematic and purely rational legislation, the United States tends to legislate on specific issues. The classification of these six measures corresponds to hot topics in legislation and policy, including food donation, animal feeding, food date labeling, food waste bans, and waste recycling. Additionally, tax incentive policies exist, but due to space constraints, this document does not elaborate further on them (Fig. 2.14).

Firstly, there are provisions related to food labeling. The federal *Food, Drug, and Cosmetic Act* requires food packaging and marketing not to include "false labeling".[35] Such "false labeling" may lead to food waste as it may not meet consumers' expectations and result in more food waste.[36] Although the law imposes mandatory requirements for nutritional labeling, it does not cover effective date labeling which is more directly related to food waste. Products without clear expiration dates are more likely to be discarded. In fact, there are no mandatory federal requirements for food date labeling, except for infant formula, which must be labeled with "use by" dates determined through experimentation; otherwise, it would be illegal.[37] States and local regulations on food date labeling vary. Due to different emphases, there are

[32] Adam Chandler, "Why Americans Lead the World in Food Waste," *Atlantic*, July 15, 2016, https://www.theatlantic.com/business/archive/2016/07/american-food-waste/491513/.

[33] Suzanne Goldenberg, "Half of All US Food Produce Is Thrown Away, New Research Suggests," *The Guardian*, July 13, 2016, https://www.theguardian.com/environment/2016/jul/13/us-food-waste-ugly-fruit-vegetables-perfect?CMP=share_btn_tw.

[34] U.S. Environmental Protection Agency, "Wasted Food Programs and Resources Across the United States," https://www.epa.gov/sustainable-management-food/wasted-food-scale.

[35] U.S. Government Publishing Office, *Public Health Service Act*, https://www.govinfo.gov/content/pkg/COMPS-973/pdf/COMPS-973.pdf.

[36] K. B. Gines, "Food Waste: Regulatory Game?" *Drake Journal of Agricultural Law* 24, no. 1 (2019): 97–116.

[37] 21 CFR 107.20(c) (2023).

Fig. 2.14 Wasted Food Scale (Adapted from EPA, US 2023)

significant differences in labeling requirements and date terminology. For example, terms like “use by,” “sell by,” and “best before” are commonly used, leading to consumer confusion between quality and safety of the food. California has date labeling requirements for dairy products, eggs, and shellfish, but it does not directly prohibit the sale or donation of food beyond labeled date.[38] Other states mostly have date labeling requirements for shellfish, dairy products, eggs, and similar items. Additionally, some states may impose restrictions on the sale or donation of specific types of food after the labeled date, but generally, restrictions on selling after date food are stricter than restrictions on donating it.

Secondly, there are liability and safety provisions regarding donated food. The most important law in reducing food waste at its source and in recycling stages is

[38] CAL. FOOD & AGRIC. CODE § 36004; CAL. CODE REGS. TIT. III, § 627; CAL. HEALTH & SAFETY CODE § 114039; CAL. FOOD & AGRIC. CODE § 82000-1; CAL. HEALTH & SAFETY CODE § 114057; CAL. FOOD & AGRIC. CODE § 27644.

the federal Good Samaritan Food Donation Act of 1996.[39] This law aims to protect various types of goodwill food donors, such as individuals and nonprofit organizations that receive and distribute donated food, by providing conditional civil and criminal liability exemptions. However, it's worth noting that besides specific legal provisions, the U.S. Congress has never designated any federal agency to enforce this law (Huang and Xi 2021) In contrast, some states in the U.S. have enacted more comprehensive rules on food donation. For instance, in addition to the federal law, California provides additional provisions stating that even food past its labeled date may be exempt from liability if the distributor acknowledges that there are no quality issues.

Virginia goes further by providing civil and criminal liability exemptions for food donors and food organizations even if the food does not comply with legal date labeling, as long as all parties are informed.[40] The Good Samaritan Food Donation Act sets a baseline for state legislation on liability exemptions for food donations. Some states have expanded the scope of liability exemptions based on this baseline to further incentivize food donation activities. However, the existence of liability exemptions for food donation does not mean relinquishing control over the safety of donated food. On the contrary, most states have regulations on packaging, storage, and transportation conditions for donated food. Texas has strict requirements for the safety of donated food, stating that packaged food must be refrigerated at temperatures below 5 degrees Celsius throughout the donation process, while non-packaged or opened food must also meet temperature control requirements; otherwise, it cannot be donated.[41] In addition to specifying storage and transportation conditions for eligible donated food types, Washington State has developed detailed donation guidelines for various food types to ensure food safety.[42]

Thirdly, there are several provisions on animal feed. The practice of using food waste as animal feed was once very popular in the United States, but such practices can easily lead to outbreaks of diseases in livestock, especially when animal residues are used as feed, which can lead to outbreaks of diseases such as mad cow disease. Consequently, related regulations on using food waste as animal feed have been enacted. At the federal level, the Swine Health Protection Act of 1980 requires that food residues used as pig feed must be free of pathogenic bacteria. Licensed or permitted food residue feeders are also required to heat-treat prescribed feed to prevent disease outbreaks.[43] The FDA's 1997 Bovine Spongiform Encephalopathy Feed Ban prohibits the inclusion of mammalian materials such as pork and beef in feed to prevent outbreaks of bovine spongiform encephalopathy. It also sets requirements for processing, labeling, and traceability of materials that may contain

---

[39] U.S. Congress, House of Representatives, *Report 104–661—Committee on Appropriations*, 104th Congress, https://www.congress.gov/104/crpt/hrpt661/CRPT-104hrpt661.pdf.

[40] VA. CODE ANN. § 3.2-5144.

[41] 25 TEX. ADMIN. CODE § 228.64.

[42] Wash. Admin. Code § 246-215-09415.

[43] U.S. Congress, House of Representatives, *H.R.6593—Swine Health Protection Act*, 96th Congress, October 17, 1980, https://www.congress.gov/bill/96th-congress/house-bill/6593.

mammalian materials.[44] The FDA Food Safety Modernization Act of 2011 includes specific provisions on preventive control of livestock feed, regulating food waste feed in particular. Livestock feed processing plants must take measures to prevent food-borne diseases from spreading in livestock. Similarly, based on federal regulations, states have varying rules on food waste feed. Some states like South Dakota, Washington, D.C., and Utah have few regulations on feed made from food waste, apart from federal status, while others like Texas, Alabama, and Louisiana have stricter regulations. For instance, Texas prohibits feeding pigs with feed containing animal-sourced food and requires licenses for feeding pigs with vegetable or dairy-sourced food, albeit with exemptions for individuals.[45]

Lastly, disposal methods for organic waste recycling are subject to varying regulations primarily at the state, county, and municipal levels, reflecting the decentralized nature of federal organic waste management responsibilities. While the "Resource Conservation and Recovery Act" underscores that solid waste disposal remains chiefly the purview of states and localities, it also acknowledges the emergence of solid waste issues as a national concern.[46] Most states lack mandatory regulations regarding organic waste recycling or bans, yet some jurisdictions have implemented stringent recycling mandates mandating classification and collection. For instance, California requires food waste generators to donate eligible items and arrange for recycling of the remainder, with jurisdictions obligated to provide organic waste recycling services.[47] San Francisco mandates property owners and businesses to subscribe to recycling services and individuals to participate in recycling programs.[48] Vermont mandates organic waste classification and recycling for all entities,[49] whereas New York State mandates recycling only for certain entities generating over two tons of organic waste weekly, alongside encouraging donations of eligible food.[50] New York City imposes specific regulations requiring composting, processing, or on-site handling for certain organic waste generators.[51] Composting emerges as a key aspect, integrated into landfill ban regulations, with large-scale producers required to compost or utilize composting facilities to prevent direct landfilling or incineration of organic waste. Specific requirements regarding landfilling at the federal level are primarily enforced by the Environmental Protection Agency (EPA) under the 1996 Land Disposal Flexibility Act. According to the rules specified under this Act, monitoring measures for landfill gas are only required post-closure of the landfill.[52] Operators or owners are obligated to take measures to prevent harm to human

[44] U.S. Congress, House of Representatives, *H.R.2751—FDA Food Safety Modernization Act*, 111th Congress, January 4, 2011, https://www.congress.gov/bill/111th-congress/house-bill/2751.

[45] TEX. AG. CODE ANN. §§ 165.001, 165.026; TEX. ADMIN. CODE TIT. 4, § 55.3.

[46] See 42 U.S.C. § 6901(a)(4) (2022).

[47] CAL. CODE REGS. TIT. XIV, § 18981.1–18998.4.

[48] S.F. ENV. CODE §§ 1901–1912.

[49] VT. STAT. ANN. TIT. 10, § 6605 K.

[50] N.Y. ENVTL. CONSERVATION LAW §§ 27-2201–27-2219.

[51] N.Y.C. ADMIN. CODE § 16-306.1.

[52] 40 CFR 258.61(a) (2023).

health only when methane landfill gas emissions exceed 25% of the lower explosive limit.[53] The collection and handling of methane landfill gas are governed by the Clean Air Act, which imposes requirements on landfills of certain capacities to setup landfill gas collection and control system. California situates regulations concerning methane landfill gas under the subsection of climate change within the jurisdiction of air resources. Beyond mandating landfill owners and operators to monitor landfill gas, specific landfill facilities of certain capacities are obligated to construct gas collection facilities, more detailed provisions are outlined for proposal submission, facility construction, and incineration emission standards, as well as legal responsibilities.[54]

2.4.2.2 Congressional Bills and Other Measures

The United States Congress introduces numerous bills concerning organic waste-related issues, yet a majority remain at the proposed bill without achieving legal status. For instance, during the 117th Congress, out of 17,817 bills and resolutions, only 365 bills were passed and enacted.[55] Despite the limited number of enacted legislation, they shed light on legislators' concerns and legislative trends in organic waste management. Notable proposals include the "*Food Recovery Act*" of 2017, which aimed to reduce food waste through source reduction, donation, and recycling methods. Additionally, the "*Zero Food Waste Act*" proposed during the 117th Congress sought federal funding for projects and research focused on reducing food waste.[56] Other proposals, such as the "*Food Date Labeling Act*" and the "*Compost Act*" targeted issues like inconsistent date labeling and improving composting infrastructure,[57,58] indicating a growing legislative interest in tackling food waste at various stages of the supply chain.

At the federal level, the Environmental Protection Agency (EPA) and the United States Department of Agriculture (USDA) have collaborated to set ambitious goals for food waste reduction by 2030. Initiatives like the "*Winning on Reducing Food Waste*" Initiative aim to achieve a 50% reduction in food waste and disposal by 2030 through interdepartmental cooperation. This initiative outlines strategies such as enhancing interagency coordination, strengthening consumer education, improving

---

[53] 40 CFR 258.23(a) (2023).

[54] Cal. Admin. Code tit. 17, § 95460-95476.

[55] Govtrack.us, "Definition of Enacted Legislation: Enacted Bills That Were Either Signed by the President or Enacted via a Veto Override or the 10-Day Rule (Including Joint Resolutions Which Can Also Be Enacted as Law)," in *Statistics of Bills and Resolutions 117th Congress*, https://www.govtrack.us/congress/bills/statistics.

[56] U.S. Congress, House of Representatives, *H.R.4444—Zero Food Waste Act*, 117th Congress, July 19, 2021, https://www.congress.gov/bill/117th-congress/house-bill/4444/text.

[57] U.S. Congress, House of Representatives, *H.R.3159—Food Date Labeling Act of 2023*, 118th Congress, June 1, 2023, https://www.congress.gov/bill/118th-congress/house-bill/3159.

[58] U.S. Congress, House of Representatives, *H.R.651—COMPOST Act*, 118th Congress, February 23, 2023, https://www.congress.gov/bill/118th-congress/house-bill/651.

food waste assessment systems, and encouraging private sector collaboration. Partnerships with organizations like the Food Waste Reduction Alliance (FWRA) further bolster efforts, focusing on reducing food waste generation, increasing food donations, and seeking alternative solutions to disposal. Through legislative and administrative actions, policymakers are actively pursuing measures to address food waste throughout the supply chain, signaling a significant shift towards more sustainable waste management practices.

2.5 City, Business, and NGO Innovations on Food Waste

2.5.1 American Composting Association

The Institute for Local Self-Reliance (ILSR), established in 1974, is a national nonprofit research and educational organization. Its "Community Composting Initiative" focuses on promoting composting activities, which enhance local soil and community health.[59] Specifically, ILSR is dedicated to catalyzing decentralized composting options for food residuals, including methods at the household, community, and farm levels, as well as larger-scale facilities. This approach aims to empower communities in managing and utilizing organic waste while reducing reliance on traditional landfills and incinerators.

The organization's strategy not only aims to directly improve environmental quality but also to strengthen community cohesion and economic self-reliance. This multifaceted goal structure ensures the sustainability and long-term impact of the projects.

ILSR's projects display high levels of innovation and practicality in technological applications. Various composting technologies are employed, such as bin systems, turned windrow composting, and static pile methods, to suit specific community needs and environmental conditions. For example, in urban settings, enclosed bin systems are often used to prevent pests and maintain cleanliness during the composting process. These technologies are chosen with consideration for ease of operation and control over compost quality, ensuring the efficiency and sustainability of the composting activities.

ILSR actively collaborates with local governments, schools, NGOs, and community residents to promote the implementation of composting projects. This broad cooperation not only strengthens the community foundation of the projects but also enhances residents' awareness and support for sustainable waste management through direct participation. Particularly in schools and community gardens, establishing demonstration composting sites and educational activities increased environmental awareness and participation among community members, especially youths.

---

[59] Institute for Local Self-Reliance, "Community Composting," https://ilsr.org/composting/community-composters/.

From an environmental impact perspective, ILSR's community composting projects have successfully reduced the volume of organic waste entering landfills and incinerators. By converting these organic wastes into high-quality compost, the projects significantly reduce greenhouse gas emissions, particularly methane. Moreover, the use of compost improves soil structure and increases organic matter content, thus enhancing soil moisture retention and nutrient levels, which support healthier and more sustainable local vegetation growth.

On a social level, the projects enhance community cohesion through education and participation. ILSR not only provides technical training in compost production but also educates community members about the importance of sustainable waste management through public courses and seminars. This educational approach effectively raises environmental consciousness among community members and fosters intergenerational and cross-cultural dialogue and cooperation. Additionally, the projects offer volunteer opportunities that allow community members to directly participate in compost production and maintenance, enhancing their sense of self-efficacy and happiness from contributing to the community.

Economically, ILSR's community composting projects positively impact the local economy by creating jobs and reducing waste management costs. The projects provide direct employment opportunities for local residents, especially in project management, material collection, and processing. These job opportunities are often offered to marginalized groups within the community, helping to improve their economic status. Furthermore, by reducing reliance on commercial fertilizers and external soil amendments, the use of community-generated compost also helps local farmers and gardening enthusiasts reduce costs.

2.5.2 China Composting Association

The "Community Food Waste Composting Pilot Project" initiated by Nanjing University (Lishui) Institute of Ecology and Environment in collaboration with the Vanke Foundation is China's first nationwide community composting project. Launched at the end of 2018, it now encompasses nearly 50 communities across 22 cities in China, primarily in urban residential areas. In early 2024, the third phase of the community composting plan was initiated, adding 70 new community composting projects across 17 provinces.[60] This five-year pilot project demonstrates how community composting can locally close the loop on food waste and reduce methane emissions, aiding in the creation of carbon–neutral communities.

Innovative measures have been introduced in the community food waste composting pilot project implemented by Nanjing University (Lishui) Institute of

[60] Molly Bergen, "A Bottom-Up Food Waste and Climate Solution in China," *New Security Beat*, December 2023, https://www.newsecuritybeat.org/2023/12/bottom-up-food-waste-and-climate-solution-in-china/.

Ecology and Environment and the Vanke Foundation to enhance composting efficiency, promote community participation, and strengthen the impact of education and training. These innovations manifest in technical applications, community mobilization strategies, and educational and training efforts, effectively driving the implementation of the project and ensuring its sustainability.

Technologically, the project utilizes advanced composting facilities and management systems, such as automated temperature and humidity control compost bins, which not only improve the efficiency of food waste processing but also ensure optimal environmental control during composting. Additionally, the project experiments with various composting techniques, such as rapid composting and dry composting methods, which accelerate the decomposition of organic waste and shorten the composting cycle, thus enhancing processing capacity.

In terms of community participation, the project has designed an inclusive participation model that encourages and trains residents to engage in the pre-treatment, sorting, and subsequent composting of food waste. By establishing community composting working groups and appointing compost ambassadors, not only is resident participation increased, but also internal community information flow and skill transfer are enhanced, creating a self-sustaining environmental education network.

Educational and training strategies are also crucial to the project's success. The project team has developed a range of educational materials and tools, including compost operation manuals, online video tutorials, and workshops, which educate residents about the scientific principles and practical skills of composting. Moreover, the project regularly holds community lectures and interactive discussion sessions to further deepen residents' understanding and commitment to sustainable living practices.

By effectively transforming food waste into compost, the project reduces the need for landfill and incineration, thereby lowering urban operational costs and greenhouse gas emissions. This practice directly reduces environmental pollution and enhances the overall health and sustainability of ecosystems. Additionally, the application of compost as an organic fertilizer improves soil quality and promotes vegetation growth, which has long-term positive effects on urban greening and ecological restoration.

The implementation of the project has greatly enhanced community residents' environmental awareness and participation. By organizing training workshops, providing composting facilities, and offering regular feedback and support, residents practice environmental protection in their daily lives, forming positive environmental behavior patterns. This community-level participation not only strengthens internal community ties but also enhances residents' awareness and responsibility for the environmental impacts of their actions.

The project also promotes innovation and implementation of related environmental policies. Through cooperation with local governments, the project demonstrates how community infrastructure and policy support can jointly influence environmental management and resource recycling, providing a successful case study for other cities and regions. These experiences and data support broader policy discussions and improvements, fostering the formulation and execution of sustainable development strategies. As a part of the program, the Research Center for Eco-Environmental Sciences, Chinese Academy of Sciences, completed a research on the GHG emission and carbon reduction analysis for the seven studied communities, revealing that composting could be efficient way to lower the GHG emission from the municipal solid waste management.

The community food waste composting pilot project by Nanjing University (Lishui) Institute of Ecology and Environment and the Vanke Foundation has not only achieved technical and environmental success but has also made significant contributions in social mobilization, education and training, and policy advocacy. These achievements demonstrate how environmental protection projects can achieve ecological benefits while enhancing community capacity and policy support, driving overall sustainable development in society.

When comparing the community composting projects of Nanjing University (Lishui) Institute of Ecology and Environment and the Institute for Local Self-Reliance (ILSR) in the United States, we can identify their similarities and differences in aspects such as policy orientation, community participation, and technical implementation:

2.5.3 Similarities and Differences

2.5.3.1 Similarities

Consistency in Environmental Goals

Both projects emphasize reducing food waste through community composting, improving soil quality, and reducing the environmental burden of landfill and incineration.

Community Participation and Education

Both projects recognize education and community involvement as key to success. They enhance community residents' understanding of and participation in composting and sustainable environmental practices through workshops, training, and other educational activities.

2.5.3.2 Differences

Policy and Support:

Nanjing University's project receives funds from Vanke Foundation, a NGO located in Shenzhen City, and from the local government.

ILSR's project, while also seeking government support, relies more on community self-organization and resident initiative, with funding largely dependent on community fundraising, small grants, and volunteer resources. ILSR's strategy emphasizes decentralized and small-scale composting solutions and investment in education and community capacity building.

Technology and Scope of Implementation:

Nanjing University's project is conducted within a limited number of pilot communities and often uses centralized technological solutions and facilities.

ILSR's project: Covers a broad range, with diverse implementation methods, including different composting systems in schools, farms, and community gardens among various locations.

These differences reflect how each project has developed different strategies and implementation models adapted to the local conditions of their respective countries, based on policy environments, community needs, and available resources.

This article also examines the social contributions of composting through typical cases from the composting associations in China and the United States.

In Prince George's County, the organic composting facility processes over 50,000 tons of material annually, including yard trimmings and food scraps. These materials are ground and formed into long windrows. The composting process relies on precise control of the carbon-to-nitrogen ratio, temperature, humidity, and oxygen content. After about 9 months of composting and a 3-month curing period, the final products produced are Leafgro® and Leafgro GOLD®, high-quality compost products manufactured in accordance with the Maryland Department of Agriculture's regulations. The sales revenue is used to offset the costs of composting operations. The facility also specifically utilizes GORE® Cover technology, effectively controlling odors and emissions, significantly increasing throughput and recovery rates. It is reported that the composting project generates total annual revenue of $2.4 million, including sales and tips, with about $700,000 coming from compost sales, and avoids 2713 tons of carbon dioxide emissions per month, achieving both economic and environmental benefits.[61]

Since 2019, Wuxi Ji Xiang International Garden has implemented a community composting project aimed at promoting resident participation in community environmental management and advancing the resource utilization of waste segregation and organic waste. The project covers 2431 households involving about 8500 residents. Through the setup of sealed composting facilities and a resident-led participation model, the project has successfully transformed approximately 55 tons of kitchen waste, significantly improving the community's green environment (LIEE 2022).

The project not only raises residents' awareness of environmental protection but also fosters a sense of environmental responsibility in the younger generation through

[61] Prince George's County Government, "Organics Composting Facility," https://www.princegeorgescountymd.gov/departments-offices/environment/waste-recycling/facilities/organics-composting-facility.

various educational activities and practices, particularly by actively engaging children. Moreover, the project strengthens community cohesion and residents' sense of belonging through regular composting activities and community workshops.

Due to its significant community participation and environmental achievements, Ji Xiang International Garden's composting project has been included in the city's ecological civilization education base and serves as an extracurricular practice base for schools, demonstrating and promoting it to a broader community and educational venues. The successful implementation of the project showcases how resident-led environmental protection initiatives can effectively promote sustainable development and the construction of an ecological civilization within the community.

2.5.4 Transforming Food Waste into Energy

Moreover, China and the United States are actively exploring the resource utilization of food waste. Biogenic energy recovery from anaerobic digestion of food waste was an important measure for tackling the food waste recycling issue. In China, the central government supported more than one hundred pilot cities for food waste recycling, and more than 90% of the cities applied anaerobic digestion and produced biogas for recovering the biogenic energy from waste. Researchers like Wang Xuan have used thermally activated persulfate to pretreat kitchen waste and prepared kitchen waste hydrogel (FWH) through polymer cross-linking, combined with oyster shell powder to create a gel-based slow-release nitrogen fertilizer, showing good water absorption and slow-release performance. Treating kitchen waste with thermally activated persulfate achieves efficient hydrolysis within one hour, enhancing the resource utilization efficiency of kitchen waste. The gel-based slow-release nitrogen fertilizer's application in soil shows lower nitrogen leaching loss rate compared to pure urea fertilizer, effectively reducing nitrogen loss and benefiting sustainable agriculture.[62] Researchers like Zhou Jie explored an innovative method of treating kitchen waste by breeding insects to transform it into high-value products. This method utilizes the bioconversion capability of insects such as black soldier fly larvae, fly maggots, earthworms, American cockroaches, and mealworms to transform organic matter in kitchen waste into bio-protein and other useful substances. Insect transformation not only effectively degrades kitchen waste but also converts it into high-value bio-protein and other products, improving the resource utilization efficiency of kitchen waste.[63] American researchers have developed a technology to convert food waste into jet fuel, bringing the prospect of net-zero flights a step closer.

---

[62] Wang, Xuan, Yiqing Cai, Chaoqun Tan, et al. "Preparation and Performance of Gel-Based Slow-Release Nitrogen Fertilizer from Kitchen Waste Pretreated by Thermally Activated Persulfate." *Journal of Environmental Engineering* 17, no. 4 (2023): 1327–1336.

[63] Zhou, Jie, Chunzhi Zheng, Guohua Zhang, et al. "Research on the Current Situation of Kitchen Waste as Feed." *Guangdong Chemical Industry* 49, no. 24 (2022): 193–195.

They use a process called "bio-refining" to transform food waste into paraffin, which functions in airplane engines.[64]

References

Dou, X. (2015). Food Waste Generation and Its Recycling Recovery: China's Governance Mode and Its Assessment. *Fresenius Environmental Bulletin, 24*(4A), 1474–1482.

Dreyfus, G. B., Y. Xu, D. T. Shindell, D. Zaelke, and V. Ramanathan. "Mitigating Climate Disruption in Time: A Self-Consistent Approach for Avoiding Both Near-Term and Long-Term Global Warming." *Proceedings of the National Academy of Sciences* 119, no. 22 (2022). https://doi.org/10.1073/pnas.2123536119.

GMI. "Methane Emissions Data." 2022. https://www.globalmethane.org/methane-emissions-data.aspx.

Heller, M. C., Mazor, M. H., & Keoleian, G. A. (2020). Plastics in the US: Toward a Material Flow Characterization of Production, Markets, and End of Life. *Environmental Research Letters, 15*, Article 094034.

Hope, C. (2005). The Climate Change Benefits of Reducing Methane Emissions. *Climatic Change, 68*(1), 21–39.

Liu, M., Ogunmoroti, A., Liu, W., Li, M., Bi, M., Liu, W., & Cui, Z. (2022). Assessment and Projection of Environmental Impacts of Food Waste Treatment in China from Life Cycle Perspectives. *Science of the Total Environment, 807*, Article 150751.

Narevski, A. C., Novakovic, M. I., Petrovic, M. Z., Mihajlovic, I. J., Maodus, N. B., & Vujic, G. V. (2021). Occurrence of Bisphenol A and Microplastics in Landfill Leachate: Lessons from South East Europe. *Environmental Science and Pollution Research, 28*, 42196–42203.

NBSC. *China Statistical Yearbook (2019)*. National Bureau of Statistics of China (NBSC): China Statistics Press, Beijing, 2019.

Qu, S., Guan, D., Ma, Z., & Yi, X. (2019). A Study on the Optimal Path of Methane Emissions Reductions in a Municipal Solid Waste Landfill Treatment Based on the IPCC-SD Model. *Journal of Cleaner Production, 222*, 252–266.

US EPA, O. "Draft National Strategy to Prevent Plastic Pollution." Other Policies and Guidance. April 9, 2023. https://www.epa.gov/circulareconomy/draft-national-strategy-prevent-plastic-pollution

Yang, N., Zhang, H., Shao, L. M., Lü, F., & He, P. J. (2013). Greenhouse Gas Emissions During MSW Landfilling in China: Influence of Waste Characteristics and LFG Treatment Measures. *Journal of Environmental Management, 129*, 510–521.

[64] G. Haines, "The Holy Grail of Aviation: Net-Zero Flights 'On the Horizon' Say Scientists," *Positive News*, March 16, 2021, accessed March 25, 2024, https://www.positive.news/science/net-zero-flights-on-the-horizon-say-scientists/.

Chapter 3
Innovative Approaches to Reducing Plastic Pollution in the US and China

3.1 Section Summary

Research by the Organization for Economic Co-operation and Development (OECD) predicts a 70% increase in annual plastic use and waste generation by 2040 compared to 2020, driven by population growth and higher incomes. Both the United States and China have made notable efforts to mitigate this trend. As of February 2022, 11 U.S. states and various local ordinances have enacted plastic restrictions. Similarly, China has introduced comprehensive plastic management policies emphasizing full-life-cycle management of plastics. This summary examines the innovative approaches each country is taking to address plastic pollution.

3.1.1 Approaches to Plastic Usage Restrictions

Common methods for controlling plastic pollution include legislation, bans, and fines. In the US, economic interventions like taxes and fees on plastic bag usage are prevalent. Meanwhile, China highlights detailed policy formulations from central to local levels, integrating the concept of "full life cycle" management. This comprehensive approach ensures that all stages of plastic use, from production to disposal, are regulated.

3.1.2 Innovative Methods and Policies

In the US, innovation includes banning expanded polystyrene (EPS) food service products to address the issue at its raw material stage. Some states offer exemptions for public welfare programs during the transition period of new laws, reflecting

H. Huang et al., *Waste Management for Global Sustainability*, CSR, Sustainability, Ethics & Governance, https://doi.org/10.1007/978-981-96-8305-5_3

concern for disadvantaged groups. Fines collected from businesses that violate the rule on plastic ban are often used to enhance local natural and cultural environments.

China has showcased business models to incentivize plastic reuse and practical references for private reduction initiatives. Region-specific actions include Hainan Province's stringent regulations on non-biodegradable plastic products and Zhejiang Province's specific targets for plastic pollution control.

3.1.3 Obstacles in Implementation

In the US, 19 states have enacted preemption laws preventing local governments from implementing plastic restrictions, creating significant regulatory barriers. In contrast, China faces challenges in policy enforcement and effectiveness measurement across varying local implementations.

3.1.4 Top-Down and Bottom-Up Policy Reforms in China

China, the world's largest producer and consumer of plastics, has made concerted efforts to control single-use plastics (SUPs). Policies target reducing disposable plastics like bags, tableware, and packaging by setting quantifiable goals. For example, the General Office of the State Council's directive aims to ban non-biodegradable plastic straws in the food industry by the end of 2020 and reduce plastic bags in marketplaces by 2025.

3.1.5 National and Local-Level Policies in China

China's national policies cover a broad range, from the 2007 plastic bag restriction notice to the 2020 "*Opinions on Further Strengthening the Control of Plastic Pollution*". These policies promote the use of biodegradable plastics, enhance recycling, and establish long-term management mechanisms.

Research by the Organization for Economic Co-operation and Development (OECD) shows that, under the baseline scenario, current population growth trends and higher incomes will lead to a 70% increase in annual plastic use and waste generation in 2040 compared to 2020.[1] Efforts have been made in both the United States and China to limit the increase in plastic use. As of February 2022, 11 U.S. states have enacted statewide plastic restrictions, and 13 states have implemented plastic restrictions through local ordinances. In recent years, China's plastic management policies

[1] OECD, Towards Eliminating Plastic Pollution by 2040. A Policy Scenario Analysis. November 2023.

have also been introduced, ranging from clarifying the top-level design of plastic governance to implementing departmental functions and emphasizing full-life-cycle management of plastics. China's Hainan Province, some local enterprises and private organizations, also have many innovations in response to plastic governance.

In terms of approach, the common ways for plastic usage restrictions are legislation, bans, and setting fines. Secondly, the method of controlling plastic pollution in the states of the United States is more inclined to use economic means to intervene in the use of plastic bags, such as levying taxes and charging for the use of plastic bags. China pays more attention to the formulation of policies, from the central to local implementation of policy implementation details, in the management of plastic policy highlights the concept of "full life cycle" management.

In addition, China and the United States, in part of their innovative approach, also made a useful attempt. Some states in the United States prohibit companies from distributing food service products made from expanded polystyrene (EPS), initiating intervention from the raw material use stage of plastics. During the transition period of the law implementation, the bills of some U.S. states also reflect the concern for the disadvantaged groups in the plastic restriction by exempting the public welfare programs from the use fee. Finally, in the use of fines, some U.S. states collect fines from companies that violate the directive on the ban on the use of plastic, which will be used to target the maintenance and enhancement of local natural and cultural environments and used to bridge the impacts caused by plastic pollution. Some regions in China have put forward business models to incentivize reuse and practical references for plastic reduction initiatives, which provide reference examples for various stakeholders in the plastic industry chain in solving the plastic problem.

However, both countries also face different obstacles. As of February 2022, 19 states in the United States have prevented local governments from enacting plastic restrictions through preemption, and eight states do not have regulations related to plastic bags.[2] Nineteen states currently exercise state preemption to prevent lower-level counties, cities, and other local governments from enacting plastic restrictions. The effectiveness of China's policy implementation from the central to the local level has yet to be formulated by a corresponding evaluation system to respond to the effectiveness of the policy in terms of actual plastic reduction.

3.2 Snapshot of Chinese Top-Down and Bottom-Up policy Reforms on SUPs

China is the world's largest producer of plastics and the largest consumer of plastic products. In order to deal with the plastic problem, the Chinese government has introduced a series of policies since 1999 to gradually strengthen the control of

[2] PlasticBagLaws.org, "Preemption," https://www.plasticbaglaws.org/preemption.

single-use plastic products.[3] In China's latest national program, the 14th Five-Year Plan, a more comprehensive plastic pollution control policy has been enacted, with a timeline for the control of key plastic products, with a focus on the reduction of disposable plastic products such as plastic bags, plastic tableware, courier packaging, and agricultural films.

In terms of quantitative targets, the Opinions on Further Strengthening the Control of Plastic Pollution issued by the General Office of the State Council of China (GuoBanFa [2020] No. 50), which clearly defined the overall requirements, key tasks, and supporting policies for China's plastic pollution control, proposed that by the end of 2020, the use of non-biodegradable single-use plastic straws will be banned from the food and beverage industry; and by the end of 2022, hotels nationwide, By the end of 2022, hotels and other venues will no longer actively provide disposable plastic products, and the use of non-biodegradable plastic bags will be prohibited in marketplaces; by the end of 2025, it will take the lead in banning and restricting the production, sale and use of some plastic products in some regions and some fields.[4]

3.2.1 China's National Level Policies

China's measures to combat plastic pollution cover a wide range of levels, including policy, business and public awareness and education. Relevant policies have been introduced in recent years, including a comprehensive ban on waste entry in 2021, the issuance of the "*Circular on the 14th Five-Year Plan of Action on Plastic Pollution Control*", the definition of microplastics as a new pollutant in 2022, and the issuance of the "*Measures for the Administration of the Use and Reporting of Disposable Plastic Products by Operators in the Business Sector*" in 2023, among others, which promote the action on plastic pollution control in China. Plastic Pollution Control Action. In order to further strengthen the management of plastic pollution, the government has also formulated and implemented the "14th Five-Year Plan" Action Program for Plastic Pollution Management, which aims to strengthen the management of plastic pollution and establish a sound economic system for low-carbon and recycling development.

At the national level, China has formulated a series of policies and regulations to prevent and control plastic pollution and promote the development of circular economy. As early as 2007, China introduced its first policy to limit the use of plastic bags, the *Notice on Restrictions on the Production, Sale and Use of Plastic Shopping Bags* issued by the General Office of the State Council. In China's large shopping

[3] Aqsa T. Malik et al., "Implementation of Enhanced Recovery after Surgery Protocol for Total Hip Arthroplasty Results in Reduced Length of Hospital Stay, Reduced 30-Day Readmission Rates, and Improved Postoperative Pain Scores," *Journal of Orthopaedic Surgery and Research* 16, no. 1 (2021), https://www.ncbi.nlm.nih.gov/pmc/articles/PMC8418295/.

[4] Lingzhi Ren et al., "An Overview of Management Status and Recycling Strategies for Plastic Packaging Waste in China," *Recycling* 8, no. 6 (2023): 90, https://www.mdpi.com/2313-4321/8/6/90.

malls and supermarkets, measures have been gradually implemented to pay for the use of plastic bags, but in some cities and rural areas, the policy of restricting the use of disposable plastic bags has not been thoroughly implemented; in recent years, with China's emphasis on the recycling economy, garbage classification, renewable resources utilization and other work, various ministries and commissions have issued policies and measures closely related to the recycling and utilization of plastic waste, such as the "*Specification Conditions for the Comprehensive Utilization of Waste Plastics Industry*". The Chinese government has adopted a variety of measures, such as the number of sources, cleaning and recycling of plastic waste, harmless disposal, banning and restricting the use of certain plastic products, and the establishment of a long-term management mechanism, etc. The Chinese government also encourages the recycling of plastic waste by a variety of means, such as the number of sources, cleaning and recycling of plastic waste, harmless disposal, banning and restricting the use of certain plastic products, and the establishment of a long-term management mechanism. The Chinese government also encourages the reduction of the use of plastic products, especially in terms of plastic packaging and disposable plastic products, and promotes the use of biodegradable or recyclable materials as substitutes. At the same time, the recovery rate and level of recycling of plastic waste are being strengthened in order to promote the recycling of resources. For plastic wastes that are difficult to recycle, the policy requires harmless disposal in sanitary landfills and incinerators. In addition, the government prohibits and restricts the use of certain plastic products, such as non-compliant plastic microbeads and ultra-thin agricultural films; in January 2020, the National Development and Reform Commission (NDRC) and the Ministry of Ecology and Environment (MOE) jointly issued the *Opinions on Further Strengthening the Control of Plastic Pollution*, which plans to establish a management system for plastic products that includes the production, distribution, consumption and recycling and disposal of plastic products, and to promote plastic substitution products to significantly reduce plastic Garbage pollution, China's most stringent "plastic restriction" and plastic pollution prevention and control policy in history.[5]

3.2.2 Local-Level Policies in China

With the promotion of China's "Plastic Restriction Order", Beijing, Hebei, Heilongjiang, Jilin, Jiangsu, Zhejiang, Fujian, Guangdong, Sichuan and other provinces and cities have responded positively and put forward a series of targeted key tasks and policy measures.

Hainan Province has issued the "Hainan Province prohibit the transportation of non-biodegradable plastic products from outside the province into the island special

[5] "China Tightens Controls on Use of Plastics," *The State Council of the People's Republic of China*, last modified May 11, 2020, https://english.www.gov.cn/policies/policywatch/202005/11/content_WS5eb88dd4c6d0b3f0e94975b3.html.

rectification work program", "Hainan Special Economic Zone prohibit disposable non-biodegradable plastic products regulations", "on the promotion of Hainan Province e-commerce platforms to ban plastic a number of measures," and other related policy documents, a clear ban on the production and sale of disposable non-biodegradable plastic shopping bags, tableware, disposable plastic drinking straws, and other products. It has strengthened the management and supervision of the production, sale and use of plastic products, strictly enforced the relevant laws and regulations, increased the penalties for non-compliance, encouraged and supported the recycling and reuse of recycled plastic resources, promoted the development of circular economy, and strengthened the publicity and education of public environmental protection awareness, guided the residents to reduce the use of plastic products, and advocated green consumption and lifestyles.

Zhejiang Province has issued the "Implementation Measures on Further Strengthening the Control of Plastic Pollution", which puts forward specific targets for the control of plastic pollution. Sichuan Province issued the Implementation Measures on Further Strengthening the Control of Plastic Pollution, which put forward 16 key tasks and safeguard measures, such as strengthening the control of the source, strengthening the standardization and management, perfecting the standard system, and expanding alternative products. Beijing Municipality has issued the *Beijing Municipal Domestic Waste Management Regulations* and *the Beijing Municipal Plastic Pollution Control Action Plan*, which prohibit the use of ultra-thin plastic bags in retail establishments and do not provide plastic bags for free, and also set plastic reduction targets for six key industries such as wholesale and retail of catering and takeout platforms. Shanghai has issued the *Shanghai Municipal Domestic Waste Management Regulations*, the *Shanghai Municipal Implementation Plan on Further Strengthening the Treatment of Plastic Pollution*, the *Implementation Opinions on Further Strengthening the Treatment of Plastic Pollution* in the city, the Shanghai Municipal Implementation Plan on Further Strengthening the Treatment of Plastic Pollution in the Business Sector, and the Shanghai Municipal Action Plan for the Treatment of Plastic Pollution (2022–2025), which specifies the Shanghai's plastic pollution control in the next few years, the objectives, key tasks and safeguard measures, put forward to strengthen the management of domestic waste, clarify the timetable and scope of banning the use of or restricting the use of disposable plastic products, and clarify the specific measures and requirements for plastic pollution control. Jilin Province introduced the "Jilin Province prohibit the sale and use of disposable non-biodegradable plastic bags, plastic tableware regulations" marking the Jilin Province from January 1, 2015 began to formally implement the "ban on plastics", which also became China's implementation of the "Plastic Restriction Order" 6 years since, the first comprehensive "plastic ban". The first comprehensive "plastic ban" in the province, as well as the 2023 release of the "CPC Jilin Provincial Committee of the Jilin Provincial People's Government on the depth of the implementation of pollution prevention and control of the implementation of the views" clearly put forward to strictly implement the requirements of the ban on plastics and the implementation of the recovery of agricultural film, pesticide packaging action, Jilin Province, also plans to 2025, the postal courier outlets Jilin Province also plans to prohibit the use of non-degradable plastic packaging by 2025, accelerating the construction of "waste-free city".

All in all, China's policy on plastic management is a comprehensive and systematic system, including plastic restriction policy, plastic ban policy, promoting the use of biodegradable plastics, strengthening the recycling of waste plastics and other aspects, covering all aspects from source reduction to recycling and reuse. The implementation of these policies will help to reduce plastic pollution, promote the green transformation of the plastics industry and facilitate environmental protection and sustainable development.

3.2.3 Chinese Civil Society Policy Advocacy on Plastic Waste Management

In the advocacy of plastic pollution management and reduction, local Chinese civil society organizations and enterprises have made many useful attempts. They actively advocate that the concepts of full life cycle management of plastics and circular economy should be incorporated into policies, and have put forward their outlook on international and domestic plastics policies, including incentivizing business models for reuse, strengthening technical specifications for green design, improving policy synergies across the entire plastics industry chain, and paying more attention to the establishment of a reuse system and recognizing the urgency of its establishment, which provide reference value for all stakeholders in the plastics industry chain. The outlook of international and domestic plastics policies, such as paying more attention to the establishment of reuse system and recognizing the urgency of its establishment, provides reference value for all stakeholders of the plastics industry chain.

Relevant studies show that in China, if we aim to phase out single-use plastics, assuming that 40% of the reduction will come from reuse systems, combined with comprehensive solutions, by 2040 it is expected that the production of new plastics in the packaging industry will be reduced from 79 million tons to 9 million tons. By 2040, carbon emissions from the packaging industry are expected to decrease from 375 million tons to 156 million tons, a 58% reduction.[6]

[6] Global "Plastics Pact" Negotiations Underway, Plastic Pollution Control Multi-Party Practices in China. https://baijiahao.baidu.com/s?id=1797192581011624607&wfr=spider&for=pc.

3.3 Snapshot of US (Including STATE-Level) Policy Reforms on SUPs

3.3.1 U.S. Federal-Level Laws and Policies

In the United States, over 500 local governments and 12 states have enacted laws to control plastic pollution, including bans on plastic bags, charges for carryout bags, and restrictions on items like straws, food ware, and to-go cups.[7] While comprehensive federal legislation specifically targeting single-use plastics has not yet been established, federal efforts have been directed towards encouraging international cooperation to manage plastic waste, improving recycling and waste management infrastructure, and promoting voluntary industry actions to reduce plastic pollution. Recently, the federal government has made significant strides in tackling the environmental impacts of SUPs and enhancing recycling efforts, reflecting a broader commitment to reducing plastic pollution, fostering sustainability, and promoting a circular economy for plastics.

3.3.1.1 Biden Administration's Commitment

The Biden administration has shown a strong commitment to addressing the issues related to single-use plastics. Federal agencies have been directed to address the environmental injustices caused by plastic pollution. President Biden's ***2023 Executive Order on Environmental Justice, Revitalizing Our Nation's Commitment to Environmental Justice for All***, directs every federal agency to "make achieving environmental justice part of its mission," explicitly calling on them to "identify, analyze, and address disproportionate and adverse human health and environmental effects (including risks) and hazards of Federal activities".[8] This directive focuses explicitly on reducing plastic pollution that impacts vulnerable communities and ecosystems.

Also, single-use plastics contribute significantly to environmental and climate-related issues. They are a substantial, though often overlooked, contributor to climate change. If plastic production and use continue to grow as projected, by 2030, associated greenhouse gas emissions could reach 1.34 gigatons per year, comparable to the emissions from hundreds of new coal-fired power plants.[9] To reduce greenhouse gas emissions comprehensively, President Biden's ***2021 Executive Order on Catalyzing Clean Energy Industries and Jobs Through Federal Sustainability (EO***

---

[7] C. Meiffren-Swango, J. Engstrom, and L. Sokolow, "Plastic Bag Bans Work," *Environment America*, January 17, 2024, https://environmentamerica.org/center/resources/plastic-bag-bans-work/.

[8] Executive Office of the President, "Executive Order 14096: Revitalizing Our Nation's Commitment to Environmental Justice for All," *Federal Register*, April 26, 2023, https://www.federalregister.gov/documents/2023/04/26/2023-08955/revitalizing-our-nations-commitment-to-environmental-justice-for-all.

[9] Shen et al., "Microplastic Crisis."

14,057) tasks the federal government with significantly reducing these emissions in the coming decades. This order emphasizes a whole-of-government approach to demonstrate how innovation and environmental stewardship can protect the planet and safeguard federal investments against climate change impacts.[10] The Executive Order includes explicit mandates for agencies to minimize waste, including generating wastes that require treatment and disposal, and to advance pollution prevention. Agencies are also directed to reduce emissions, promote environmental stewardship, support resilient supply chains, drive innovation, and incentivize markets for sustainable products and services by prioritizing items that can be reused, refurbished, or recycled.

The Biden administration has significantly emphasized addressing the environmental and climate impacts of single-use plastics. Through executive orders and federal directives, the administration is taking concrete steps to reduce plastic pollution, minimize greenhouse gas emissions, and promote sustainability. These actions reflect a broader commitment to environmental justice and protecting vulnerable communities and ecosystems.

3.3.1.2 Federal Policy on Single-Use Plastics (SUPs)

When it comes to specific policies, the federal government has taken significant steps to reduce the use of plastic bags at the source. These measures aim to address the broader issue of plastic pollution by targeting some of the most prevalent single-use plastic items.

One of the most notable federal actions to reduce plastic pollution is the ***Microbead-Free Waters Act of 2015***. This legislation explicitly targets microbeads—small plastic particles commonly used in personal care products such as exfoliating scrubs and toothpaste. Recognizing the detrimental effects of microbeads on aquatic environments, the Act banned the manufacture of rinse-off cosmetics containing plastic microbeads effective July 1, 2017, and their sale from July 1, 2018.[11] This ban marked a significant step in federal efforts to reduce plastic pollution at its source, preventing these non-biodegradable particles from entering waterways where they pose a threat to marine life and ecosystems.

The ***Save Our Seas 2.0 Act***, enacted in 2020, further underscores the federal government's commitment to addressing plastic pollution. This legislation builds on the original Save Our Seas Act by enhancing the United States' ability to respond to marine debris through improved waste management practices and international collaboration. It provides funding for research and innovation in waste management

[10] Executive Office of the President, "Executive Order No. 14057: Catalyzing Clean Energy Industries and Jobs Through Federal Sustainability," *Federal Register*, December 13, 2021, https://www.federalregister.gov/documents/2021/12/13/2021-27114/catalyzing-clean-energy-industries-and-jobs-through-federal-sustainability.

[11] Rep. Pallone, "All Info - H.R.1321 - 114th Congress (2015-2016): Microbead-Free Waters Act of 2015," *Legislation*, December 28, 2015, https://www.congress.gov/bill/114th-congress/house-bill/1321/all-info.

technologies and encourages global partnerships to combat ocean plastic pollution. The Act aims to mitigate the impacts of plastic waste on marine environments and promotes a more integrated approach to managing plastic waste.[12]

In addition to these existing laws, federal legislators have introduced more comprehensive measures. For example, Senator Jeff Merkley introduced the ***Break Free from Plastic Pollution Act***. This proposed bill addresses the broader issue of plastic waste by implementing a nationwide ban on certain single-use plastics like plastic bags and straws. Moreover, it includes provisions for extended producer responsibility (EPR), which would require manufacturers to take greater accountability for the entire lifecycle of their plastic products. Although this bill has yet to become law, it represents a comprehensive approach to tackling plastic pollution by reducing production and encouraging the development of more sustainable packaging solutions.[13]

The Environmental Protection Agency (EPA) has also played a significant role in addressing plastic pollution. The ***EPA's Draft National Strategy*** to Prevent Plastic Pollution emphasizes the need for national actions to reduce the production and consumption of single-use, unrecyclable, or frequently littered plastic products. This strategy aligns with other federal policies and furthers their objectives by promoting reusable alternatives and other efforts to prevent marine debris.[14]

3.3.1.3 Federal Policy on Plastic Recycling

Efforts to improve plastic recycling at the federal level have also gained momentum. ***The Resource Conservation and Recovery Act (RCRA)*** provides the framework for managing hazardous and non-hazardous solid waste, including plastics (Rep. Pallone 2015). Recent amendments and enforcement efforts under RCRA have increasingly focused on recycling and waste minimization, reflecting a growing recognition of the need to enhance the efficiency of recycling systems.[15]

In 2020, the Environmental Protection Agency (EPA) launched the ***National Recycling Strategy***. This strategy aims to create a more resilient and effective recycling system by reducing contamination in the recycling stream, increasing the efficiency of recycling processes, and expanding markets for recycled materials. The goal is to foster a more sustainable approach to managing plastic waste, ensuring that more

---

[12] Sen. Sullivan, "Text - S.1982 - 116th Congress (2019-2020): Save Our Seas 2.0 Act," *Legislation*, December 18, 2020, https://www.congress.gov/bill/116th-congress/senate-bill/1982/text.

[13] Sen. Merkley, "Titles - S.3127 - 118th Congress (2023–2024): Break Free From Plastic Pollution Act of 2023," *Legislation*, October 25, 2023, https://www.congress.gov/bill/118th-congress/senate-bill/3127/titles.

[14] US Environmental Protection Agency. "Draft National Strategy to Prevent Plastic Pollution." Other Policies and Guidance. April 9, 2023. https://www.epa.gov/circulareconomy/draft-national-strategy-prevent-plastic-pollution.

[15] United States Government Accountability Office. *Building on Existing Federal Efforts Could Help Address Cross-Cutting Challenges*. Report to Congressional Requesters. United States Government Accountability Office, 2020. https://www.gao.gov/assets/d2187.pdf.

plastic materials are recycled and repurposed rather than ending up in landfills or the environment, and finally support the implementation of the National Recycling Goal to increase the recycling rate to 50 percent by 2030.[16]

Complementing these efforts is the ***Plastics Innovation Challenge*** initiated by the US Department of Energy. This initiative seeks to accelerate innovations in energy-efficient plastics recycling technologies and to develop new types of plastics that can be recycled more effectively. By promoting advanced recycling technologies and fostering public–private partnerships, the Plastics Innovation Challenge aims to address the technical and economic barriers to effective plastic recycling ("Strategy for Plastics Innovation", n.d.). Additionally, the federal government has supported various programs to improve recycling infrastructure and capacity. For instance, the RECYCLE Act, introduced in Congress, aims to provide grants to improve recycling education and outreach, thereby increasing public awareness and participation in recycling programs. These initiatives are designed to enhance the overall effectiveness of the US recycling system and promote a circular economy for plastics.[17]

3.3.1.4 Challenges

Despite these significant policy reforms, several challenges remain in the federal approach to managing plastic pollution and recycling. One major challenge is the fragmented nature of the US recycling infrastructure, which varies widely across states and municipalities.[18] Federal initiatives often aim to support local and state efforts to enhance recycling infrastructure and capacity, addressing inconsistencies and inefficiencies in the system.

Another challenge is the need for greater industry involvement in managing plastic waste. Policies such as extended producer responsibility (EPR) are designed to shift the burden of waste management from consumers and municipalities to producers, encouraging manufacturers to design more sustainable products and packaging. However, implementing EPR policies at the federal level requires overcoming significant political and industry resistance.[19]

---

[16] US Environmental Protection Agency. "National Recycling Strategy." Reports and Assessments. November 13, 2019. https://www.epa.gov/circulareconomy/national-recycling-strategy.

[17] Sen. Portman, "S.923 - 117th Congress (2021-2022): RECYCLE Act of 2021," *Legislation*, March 23, 2021, https://www.congress.gov/bill/117th-congress/senate-bill/923.

[18] C. Blanco, C. Spanbauer, and S. Stienecker, "America's Broken Recycling System," *California Management Review Insights*, May 2023, https://cmr.berkeley.edu/2023/05/america-s-broken-recycling-system/.

[19] Weiss, Julia I. "Extended Producer Responsibility and the Environmental Policy Implementation Process in California: A Case Study of Paintcare." Master's Thesis, San Jose State University, San Jose, CA, USA, 2019. https://doi.org/10.31979/etd.mm8b-bv86.

Public–private partnerships also play a crucial role in addressing plastic pollution. By fostering collaboration between government, industry, and non-profit organizations, these partnerships can drive innovation and promote sustainable practices in plastic production and recycling.

3.3.1.5 Conclusion

Efforts to improve plastic recycling, such as the National Recycling Strategy and the Plastics Innovation Challenge, demonstrate a concerted push to enhance recycling infrastructure, reduce contamination, and foster innovation in recycling technologies. These measures aim to create a more resilient and effective recycling system, ensuring that more plastic materials are recycled and repurposed rather than ending up in landfills or polluting the environment.

Despite these advancements, challenges remain. The fragmented nature of the US recycling infrastructure, the need for greater industry involvement, and political and industry resistance to policies like extended producer responsibility pose significant hurdles. However, by fostering public–private partnerships and encouraging sustainable practices, the federal government can continue to drive progress in managing plastic waste.

In summary, the federal government's actions reflect a growing recognition of the urgent need to address plastic pollution. The United States is taking meaningful steps toward a more sustainable future through comprehensive legislation, strategic initiatives, and collaborative efforts. As these policies evolve, they will be crucial in shaping the nation's approach to plastic waste management and environmental conservation.

3.3.2 Enactment of Bills and Policies at the State Government Level

The distribution of about one trillion single-use plastic bags around the world each year has caused many environmental problems, including harmful impacts on human and animal health; pollution of landscapes, soil, and groundwater; and increased challenges for waste management.[20] According to the U.S. Environmental Protection Agency (2020), in 2018, about 4.20 million tons of plastic waste (bags, sacks, and wraps) were generated in the United States, but only about 0.42 million tons or 10%

---

[20] E. Teuten, J.M. Saquing, D.R.U. Knappe, M.A. Barlaz, S. Jonsson, A. Björn, S.J. Rowland, R.C. Thompson, T.S. Galloway, R. Yamashita, D. Ochi, Y. Watanuki, C. Moore, P.H. Viet, T.S. Tana, M. Prudente, R. Boonyatumanond, M.P. Zakaria, K. Akkhavong, and H. Takada, "Transport and Release of Chemicals from Plastics to the Environment and to Wildlife," *Philosophical Transactions of the Royal Society B* 364 (2009): 2027–2045, https://doi.org/10.1098/rstb.2008.0284.

were recycled. For the remaining 3.78 million tons, about 0.75 million tons were combusted and 3.03 million tons were disposed of in landfills.

The distribution of more than 100 billion plastic bags every year in the United States has caused many environmental problems and an increasing number of local and state governments have enacted ordinances and legislations to ban or tax single-use plastic bags and other plastic products.[21] These measures aim to reduce plastic pollution, protect our common home and create a better environment for our future generations.

In 2007, San Francisco became the first large city in the United States to ban single-use plastic bags.[22] Washington, D.C. soon followed suit in 2009 by enacting legislation that required consumers to pay a fee of $0.05 per disposable plastic or paper bag used at checkout.[23]

Although the United States has taken very limited action at the federal level and is falling behind many European nations in addressing the environmental problems associated with plastic waste, an increasing number of state and local governments have enacted legislative interventions to ban or tax single-use plastic bags and other plastic products such as straws and "to go" cups in an effort to reduce plastic waste.[24,25] For example, after California became the first state to enact a statewide ban on single-use plastic bags in 2014, six other states (New York, Maine, Delaware, Vermont, Oregon, and Connecticut) passed laws in 2019 to ban single-use plastic bags and associated products, two more states (Washington and New Jersey) followed in 2020, and Colorado became the latest state to join the group in 2021.[26,27,28]At the municipal level, more than 300 local governments in the United States have adopted ordinances to ban or tax single-use plastic shopping bags.[29]

---

[21] Wang, Qian, Amy Tweedy, and Haoran G. Wang. "Reducing Plastic Waste Through Legislative Interventions in the United States: Development, Obstacles, Potentials, and Challenges." *Sustainable Horizons* 2 (2022): 100013. https://doi.org/10.1016/j.horiz.2022.100013.

[22] J.R. Romer, "The Evolution of San Francisco's Plastic Bag Ban," *Golden Gate University Environmental Law Journal* 4, no. 2 (2010).

[23] Xanthos, Damia, and Tony Walker. "International Policies to Reduce Plastic Marine Pollution from Single-Use Plastics (Plastic Bags and Microbeads): A Review." *Marine Pollution Bulletin* 118, no. 1–2 (2017): 17–26. https://doi.org/10.1016/j.marpolbul.2017.02.048.

[24] Wagner, Travis. "Reducing Single-Use Plastic Shopping Bags in the USA." *Waste Management* 70 (2017): 3–12. https://doi.org/10.1016/j.wasman.2017.09.003.

[25] T. Nielsen, K. Holmberg, and J. Stripple, "Need a Bag? A Review of Public Policies on Plastic Carrier Bags—Where, How, and to What Effect?" *Waste Management* 87 (2019): 429–440, https://doi.org/10.1016/j.wasman.2019.02.025.

[26] F. Nirappil, "California Becomes First State to Ban Plastic Bags," *Associated Press News*, September 30, 2014, https://apnews.com.

[27] J. Romer and L. Tamminen, "Plastic Bag Reduction Ordinances: New York City's Proposed Charge on All Carryout Bags as a Model for U.S. Cities," *Tulane Environmental Law Journal* 27, no. 2 (2014): 237–275.

[28] National Conference of State Legislators, "State Plastic and Paper Bag Legislations," *National Conference of State Legislators (NCSL)*, 2020, https://www.ncsl.org/research/environment-and-natural-resources/plastic-bag-legislation.aspx.

[29] Wagner, "Reducing Single-Use Plastic," 2017.

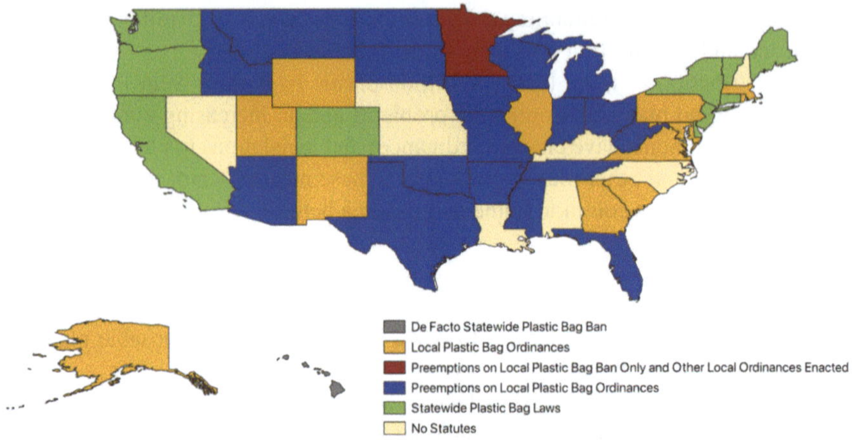

Fig. 3.1 State Plastic Bag Legislations in the US (*Source* Wang et al. [2022])

In late June 2022, the Governor of California signed SB54, which requires that all single-use packaging (including paper and metal) in the state be recyclable or compostable by January 2032, with a recycling rate of no less than 65%. This seemingly ambitious initiative aimed at transforming the plastics industry shifts the responsibility for plastic waste aftercare from the user to the producer. The new law specifies fines of up to $50,000 per day for companies that do not comply with the bill.

Figure 3.1 shows the statutes of plastic bag interventions among the 50 states in the United States. By February 2022, 11 states had enacted statewide plastic bag bans (including Hawaii with a de facto statewide ban), 13 states had implemented plastic bag interventions through local ordinances (including Minnesota which has a preemption on plastic bag bans only), 19 states had enacted preemptions that prohibit local governments from banning or regulating the use of plastic bags and other plastic products, and 8 states had no statutes on plastic bag legislations.

The statewide plastic bag interventions implemented by the 11 states in the United States have significantly different characteristics. Information reported in Table 3.1 suggests six major findings.

First, there are differences in the businesses that are covered in the plastic bag legislation across states. While the legislation in most states applies to "all businesses," including retailers and restaurants, there are exceptions for this in two states (Delaware and Colorado). For example, in Delaware, the legislation applies only to retailers with an area of more than 7000 square feet or with three or more locations with more than 3000 square feet each. The legislation also allows municipalities with populations over 50,000 to require stores with more than 500 square feet to comply. In Colorado, the legislation exempts "small stores," defined as retailers that operate solely in Colorado, have three or fewer locations, and are not part of a franchise, corporation, or partnership that has physical locations outside of Colorado.

Table 3.1 Comparison of Plastic Bag Legislations Across 11 States in the United States (Wang et al. [2022])[30]

State	Enacted date and effective date	Compliant businesses	Single-use plastic bags	Paper bags	Recipient of bag fee	Recipient of fines collected	Other related products
California	10/30/2014 7/1/2015	All	Ban	$0.10 + 123	Business	Local or state government4	
Oregon	6/20/2019 1/1/2020	All	Ban	$0.05235	Business	State	
New York	4/22/2019 3/1/2020	All	Ban	$0.0536	State/ environmental fund7	State/ environmental fund7	
Maine	6/17/2019 4/22/2020	All	Ban	≥$0.0512	Business	State	
Vermont	6/17/2019 7/1/2020	All	Ban	≥$0.101	Business	State	Expanded polystyrene plates, cups, take-out containers, straws, plastic drink stirrers
Delaware	7/29/2019 1/1/2021	Retailers with exceptions	Ban	Free	N/A	State	

(continued)

[30] (1) Must be recyclable. (2) Must be made of recycled material. (3) Customers using WIC or SNAP are exempt from paying a fee. (4) Fine collected by whichever office (local or state) brought the complaint. (5) Restaurants are not required to charge. (6) Counties and cities allowed to opt in. (7) Fees and fines collected are paid to the state and divided between an environmental fund and reusable bag distribution. (8) Fee also applies to reusable plastic bags. (9) Fee charged beginning 1/1/2021 until a ban begins on 1/1/2024. (10) 60% of fees are paid to the municipality, and 40% are retained by the business. (11) Hawaii has no statewide legislation, but four of the five counties in the state have enacted their own legislation, creating a de facto statewide ban (Hawaii's fifth county, Kalawao County, has less than 100 residents and counts for less than 0.01% of the state's population) with variations in legislation between the counties.

Table 3.1 (continued)

State	Enacted date and effective date	Compliant businesses	Single-use plastic bags	Paper bags	Recipient of bag fee	Recipient of fines collected	Other related products
Washington	3/25/2020 1/1/2021	All	Ban	$0.0828	Business	State	
Connecticut	6/26/2019 7/1/2021	All	Fee/Ban	Free	State	State	
New Jersey	11/4/2020 5/4/2022	All	Ban	Ban	N/A	Local government/ environmental fund	Expanded polystyrene plates, cups, take-out containers, plastic straws
Colorado	7/7/2021 1/1/2023	All with exceptions	Fee/Ban	$0.1023	Municipality/ Business	County	Expanded polystyrene plates, cups, take-out containers
Hawaii		All			Business	County/ environmental fund	

Second, plastic bag bans seem more popular than usage fees, likely because a ban is less complicated than charging fees for the use of plastic bags.[31] Some states also include a transition period before the ban on single-use plastic bags takes effect, charging a fee per bag in the interim. For example, Connecticut charged a fee of $0.10 per plastic bag before the state's ban took effect in July 2021 and Colorado will impose a fee from January 2021 to the end of 2023; Colorado's fee will then be replaced by a statewide ban on January 1, 2024.

Third, the regulations and requirements for paper bags vary quite a bit across the states. Six states (California, Oregon, Maine, Vermont, Washington, and Colorado) require paper bags to be recyclable, made of recycled material, or both. The same six states and the county of Honolulu require businesses to charge consumers $0.05 to $0.15 per paper bag. New York allows for counties to opt-in to requiring a fee of $0.05 per paper bag. In Maine, retail establishments are not required to charge a fee for paper bags if less than 2% of the establishment's sales are for food and it has an area of fewer than 10,000 square feet. This exception to the paper bag fee also applies to restaurants and hunger-relief organizations that distribute food to consumers at no cost. On the other hand, New Jersey considers paper bags to be single-use and has banned them alongside single-use plastic bags to reduce the emissions and energy expenditures that come with manufacturing and transporting paper bags.

Fourth, the recipient of the bag fee and the fines collected for noncompliance vary from state to state. Seven states that require a fee allow businesses to keep the revenue collected to cover the costs for implementation, distribution of paper or reusable bags, and educational materials. Meanwhile, New York and Connecticut require the bag fees collected by the businesses to be paid to the state, and Colorado requires 60% of the bag fees to be paid to the municipality or county where the businesses are located and the other 40% to be kept by the businesses. In four states, customers of the WIC (Women, Infants, and Children) program and SNAP (Supplemental Nutrition Assistance Program) are exempt from paying the bag fees. Fines for noncompliance are also paid to the state in most cases, except for in Hawaii (where each county collects the respective fine), in California (where fines are collected by the local or state office that brought the noncompliance complaint), and in Colorado (where the county in which the violation occurred collects the fee). The Maui County of Hawaii and the state of New Jersey apply the revenue collected from fines toward environmental cleanup. New York divides both the bag fees and the fines between the state's Environmental Protection Fund (60%) and a fund to help with local reusable bag distribution (40%). The plastic bag legislations in the above states also exhibit significant differences in terms of the dollar value of fines levied for violations. For example, the fines for the first violation ranged from a warning in Vermont, New York, New Jersey, and Colorado to up to $500 in Delaware. Fines for the second violation range from $25 in Vermont to up to $1,000 in Delaware and New Jersey. For subsequent offenses, fines are raised to as much as $5,000 in Delaware.

[31] Romer and Tamminen, "Plastic Bag Reduction Ordinances."

Fifth, more recent state plastic bag legislations have included plastic bags and other products. For example, Vermont, New Jersey, and Colorado have banned businesses from distributing food service products made of expanded polystyrene, a lightweight foam plastic material. They include foam cups, plates, takeout containers, egg cartons, and more. Vermont and New Jersey also require businesses to provide plastic straws only at customer request. Vermont's legislation goes even further by banning businesses from providing plastic drink stirrers as well.

Sixth, in Hawaii, the legislative interventions in the four counties with plastic ordinances have their own variations. The first county to enact legislation was Maui (2008), followed by Kauai (2009), Hawaii (2012), and Honolulu (2014). Although these four counties all banned single-use plastic bags, there are several key differences among their legislative interventions. The county of Hawaii charged a "purchase" fee for single-use plastic bags for the first year the legislation took effect and then banned single-use plastic bags after the end of the year. Also, Maui and Kauai require that paper bags be recyclable and made of recycled material. The county of Honolulu has also placed this requirement on paper bags, as well as a fee of $0.15 per paper bag, which is retained by the establishment. The fines collected for violation are paid to the respective county and, in the county of Maui, the funds are then applied toward the "*Open Space, Natural Resources, Cultural Resources, and Scenic Views Preservation Fund.*"

In addition to the above differences, there are also significant differences in the definition of single-use or reusable plastic bags. Some states base their definition solely on the thickness of the plastic bag, considering anything over 2.25 mils thick to be "reusable" or not considered as single-use, with a few states having a slightly higher requirement for the thickness of the material. In response to this definition based on the thickness, some manufacturers and retailers have been able to avoid the ban by increasing the thickness of the plastic bags being produced and distributed. States like Vermont and New Jersey have included requirements like "sewn handles" in their definition of reusable plastic bags to make it more difficult for manufacturers to continue to supply businesses with altered plastic bags to fit the definition of "reusable". In the state of Hawaii, the county of Honolulu's 2014 law required plastic bags to have a minimum thickness of 2.25 mils and be compostable before they could be considered reusable, but a new law enacted by the county in 2017 banned all bags made of plastic (compostable or otherwise), which now matches the county of Hawaii's definition.

The comparative analysis of statewide plastic legislations discussed above suggests three potential lessons for other states that are interested in developing plastic bag legislation. First, while the differences and inconsistencies in plastic bag legislations across states have caused significant confusion and costs for consumers and businesses, the states that will develop plastic bag legislations should make efforts to avoid or reduce such differences and inconsistencies with other states, especially with their neighboring states. Second, a significant transition period of at least one year between the enacted date and effective date is highly needed for consumers and businesses to understand and get prepared to comply with the legislation. Third, plastic bag legislation affects every household and many businesses, and public input and comments, from legislative bill development to legislation implementation, are needed to gain public support and participation.

References

Rep. Pallone, F. "All Info - H.R.1321 - 114th Congress (2015–2016): Microbead-Free Waters Act of 2015." *Legislation.* December 28, 2015. https://www.congress.gov/bill/114th-congress/house-bill/1321/all-info.

"Strategy for Plastics Innovation." *Energy.Gov.* Accessed June 3, 2024. https://www.energy.gov/strategy-for-plastics-innovation.

U.S. Environmental Protection Agency. "Advancing Sustainable Materials Management: 2018 Tables and Figures." 2020. https://www.epa.gov/sites/default/files/2021-01/documents/2018_tables_and_figures_dec_2020_fnl_508.pdf.

Wang, Q., A. Tweedy, and H. G. Wang. "Reducing Plastic Waste Through Legislative Interventions in the United States: Development, Obstacles, Potentials, and Challenges." *Sustainable Horizons* 2 (2022): 100013. https://doi.org/10.1016/j.horiz.2022.100013.

Chapter 4
Policy Recommendations and Potential Collaborative Efforts Between the US and China on Plastic and Food Waste Management

4.1 Section Summary

The collaboration between the US and China on waste management, particularly reducing greenhouse gas emissions from landfills and mitigating plastic and food waste pollution, holds significant promise in tackling global environmental challenges. Methane emissions from landfills represent a substantial environmental issue, contributing over 15% of total emissions in both China and the US. To address this, enhancing methane estimation accuracy and promoting landfill gas to energy (LFGTE) methods are crucial. Additionally, managing food and plastic waste is essential to reducing landfill methane emissions and fostering a sustainable future.

4.1.1 Enhancing Methods for Methane Estimation and Measurement

Initiating sophisticated research to develop accurate methane estimation models tailored to national and regional conditions is imperative. By utilizing comprehensive models based on the IPCC Tier 3 methods and sharing detailed datasets among governmental institutions, both countries can significantly improve methane emission assessments. Additionally, implementing advanced technologies to measure landfill emissions will reduce reliance on estimation models and foster innovative collaborations.

H. Huang et al., *Waste Management for Global Sustainability*, CSR, Sustainability, Ethics & Governance, https://doi.org/10.1007/978-981-96-8305-5_4

4.1.2 Promoting the Utilization of Landfill Gas (LFG)

To effectively use landfill gas as a renewable energy source, thorough investigations and efficiency evaluations of current landfill energy projects are necessary. Providing technical training for new landfill operators, along with allocating funds for research to overcome technical challenges, will ensure the sustainable operation of LFG systems. Forming collaborative partnerships with enterprises that utilize LFG can generate continuous revenue for landfill operations, while local government support through subsidies, low-interest loans, and involvement of large-scale energy enterprises can enhance project sustainability.

4.1.3 Reducing Plastics and Food Waste in Landfills

Strengthening policies to reduce plastics and food waste is critical. Implementing comprehensive legal frameworks with clear definitions and enforcement mechanisms is essential. Promoting green consumption and low-waste living through public campaigns and collaborations with NGOs, schools, and stakeholders can significantly reduce food and plastic waste.

4.1.4 Strengthening Collaborative Networks and Systems

Creating a robust collaborative network involving social partners is vital for assessing and improving municipal waste management efficiency. This includes evolving from single-stream to multi-stream recycling to reduce contamination and increase recycling rates. Enhanced cooperation among municipal, state, and federal levels will streamline waste management processes and reduce redundancies.

4.1.5 Adopting Cutting-Edge Approaches and Technologies

Large-scale adoption of composting and anaerobic digestion (AD) technologies to process food waste is urgently needed. Financial tools like low-interest loans and subsidies can support the development and implementation of these technologies. Moreover, focusing on research to improve AD and composting technologies, and exploring safe methods for plastic degradation through increased funding, will advance waste management practices.

Implementing these policy recommendations can significantly enhance cooperation between the US and China, creating effective and sustainable waste management systems. This collaboration has the potential to drastically reduce greenhouse gas emissions from landfills, minimize food and plastic waste, and foster innovation in waste management technologies. Through shared efforts, both nations can contribute to global environmental sustainability and address critical challenges posed by waste management.

4.2 Cooperation for Reducing GHG Emissions from Landfill

The methane emissions from landfills contribute over 15% of total emissions in both China and the US. To reduce the impact of landfill methane emissions, this paper suggests taking action from two aspects. First, more sophisticated and accurate estimation modeling and measurement technologies should be introduced. Second, the landfill gas to energy (LFGTE) methods should be encouraged to turn waste landfills into valuable renewable energy plants and explore new ways of collaboration among multiple parties. The following policy recommendations can apply to both China and the US scenarios.

4.2.1 Improve the Methods for Methane Estimation and Measurement

(1) Encourage more sophisticated research on estimation models. Policymakers should promote research that improves the accuracy of emission estimation results. For example, based on the IPCC Tier 3 method, China and the US can develop more comprehensive models that consider various factors influencing estimation results. Additionally, models should be tailored to each country's specific conditions. For instance, the systematic dynamic (IPCC-SD) model used by Qu et al. (2019) for estimating landfill methane emissions in China has more predictable results than the FOD methods commonly used in the US.[1] Furthermore, both China and the U.S. are now exploring the innovative monitoring method such as on-site monitoring and interpretation from satellite remote sensing images. The innovative monitoring approaches enable the two countries to precisely control the methane emissions from landfills.

(2) Promote the establishment of a comprehensive dataset and improve data sharing. Landfill emission management policymakers should facilitate the creation and sharing of detailed datasets between different government sectors and institutions. This includes sharing climate and soil data critical for estimating methane release rates. In the US, datasets from the National Climatic Data Center (NCDC) could be used to analyze landfill methane emissions. Open access to these datasets

[1] Qu et al., "Optimal Path of Methane Emissions Reductions."

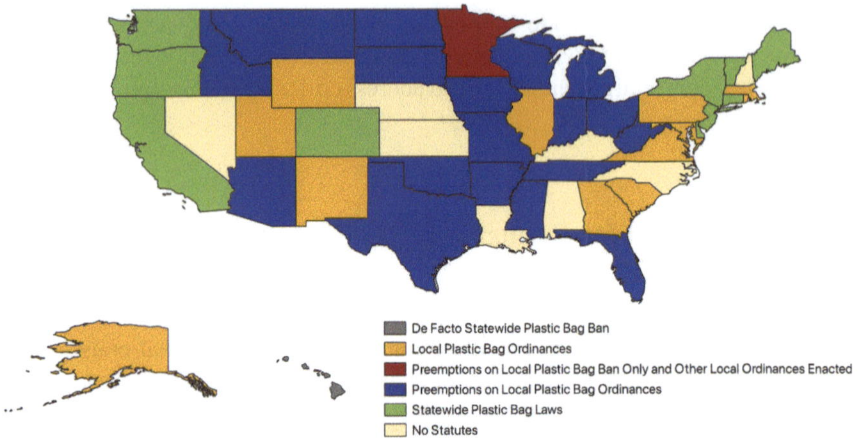

Fig. 4.1 US EPA's Landfill Methane Outreach Program (LMOP) National Map (*Source* EPA, 2022)

could also encourage volunteer involvement in measurement and data sharing, maximizing their value and ensuring they remain up-to-date. For example, the USEPA's Landfill Methane Outreach Program (LMOP) National Map includes timely updates and EJSCREEN data for project planning (Fig. 4.1).

(3) Apply advanced technologies for accurate landfill site emission measurement. Using more technologies to measure emissions can make emission factor settings more accurate and reduce reliance on estimation models. Accurate measurement approaches provide tangible results for each landfill, helping to create precise and effective policies. Additionally, this can foster collaboration among various entities, including new companies, volunteer workers, and researchers, leading to innovation and job creation.

(4) Consider the risks and costs of applying landfill-related technologies. Since landfill technologies are still in their early stages, policymakers should address the risks and costs associated with their implementation. Encouraging self-sufficient systems to make landfills profitable can support the adoption of new technologies. For example, the US EPA's Toolkit for Expiring Landfill Gas Electricity Power Purchase Agreements helps project owners understand options to keep energy projects operating and generating revenue. This revenue can incentivize landfill owners to adopt new technologies for measuring methane emissions, predicting future revenue, and fostering innovation (Table 4.1).

4.2.2 Promote the Utilization of Landfill Gas (LFG)

Given the benefits of installing energy projects in landfills, this paper provides the following suggestions to policymakers regarding utilizing landfill gas (LFG).

Table 4.1 Atmospheric and remote sensing measurements (California Air Resources Board)

Device	Measurement method
Aircraft	Aircraft to conduct area-wide flux estimates
Satellite	Satellite to show hot spots
Aircraft	Aircraft to scan sources
Tower network and inverse modeling	Tower network and inverse modeling to identify sources
Ground-based mobile monitoring	Ground-based mobile monitoring to scan local sources
Flux towers and flux chambers	Flux towers and flux chambers to measure land-based fluxes (important for landfills, dairies, rice fields, waste water)
Infrared imaging	Infrared imaging to identify sources

(1) Investigate and evaluate the efficiency of current landfill energy projects. To reduce project failure rates due to the misallocation of appropriate energy technologies, a thorough investigation and efficiency evaluation of current landfill-running energy projects should be reported. Since the oil and climate vary across different landfills, the preparation period for starting biomethanogenesis, which converts organic matter to CH_4, differs. If conditions are favorable, the bioconversion process can start in one day, with 50% of all available material converted within the first year of placement.[2] Emission efficiency also varies with landfill form, with open landfills having a collection efficiency of 70% and closed landfills slightly exceeding 80%.[3]

(2) Provide necessary technology consultancy and training for new landfill operators. Important knowledge about landfill energy projects, such as the depth of vertical wells to be drilled, well screening, collective control and monitoring systems, and piping network installation, should be included in the training. Additionally, the training should address making pipe systems easy to repair and expandable as the landfill grows.[4]

(3) Invest in research and development to overcome technological difficulties. The technical department should allocate funds and efforts to research and industrial communication to address issues that can cause landfill gas system failures, such as high leachate levels, perched water, and pipe clogging due to condensate pooling, internal fires, and corrosion due to H_2S oxidation.[5]

(4) Create collaborative partnerships for landfill gas energy projects. Landfills should seek partners to collaborate with, such as data center (DC) enterprises that use landfill gas (LFG) as a renewable energy source. This collaboration can generate

[2] N.J. Themelis and P.A. Ulloa, "Methane Generation in Landfills," *Renewable Energy* 32, no. 7 (2007): 1243–1257.

[3] Powell, Townsend, and Zimmerman, "Estimates of Solid Waste Disposal Rates."

[4] Chai, Tonjes, and Mahajan, "Methane Emissions as Energy Reservoir."

[5] Ibid.

continuous revenue for landfill operations by negotiating energy sales prices and supply modes.[6,7]

(5) Encourage local government support for LFGTE projects. Local governments should provide fiscal support for the initial establishment of landfills and promote LFGTE in subsidy lists and low-interest bank loans. Additionally, they should involve large-scale energy enterprises in LFGTE investments and construction. Large companies have the resources and experience to reduce project failure risks and can enhance the value of landfill renewable energy products, making the projects more sustainable.

4.2.3 Reduce Plastics Disposing and Food Waste in Landfills

Strengthen policies to reduce new plastic and food waste to future landfill sites. To mitigate methane emissions from landfills, efforts should focus on reducing the two most significant sources of methane: plastic and food waste. This report will discuss this issue in more detail in the next section. GHG emissions could be effectively decreased by implementing a series of interventions for promoting the recycling rate of food waste and plastic waste.

4.3 Policies Recommendations for Plastics and Food Waste Management in U.S. and China

4.3.1 Strengthen the Law and Education Systems

(1) Improve the legal system and refine norms for implementing policies against plastic and food. Despite the different systems and bodies of regulation-making in China and the US, both countries should enhance their legal frameworks by focusing on three key points: clearer definitions and law enforcement, targeting the weakest areas for effective improvement, and timely updating the legal framework to address new types of waste and pollutants.

(2) Ensure clear definitions and enforce laws with appropriate penalties and rewards. Future regulations and laws should be detailed and specific to facilitate effective enforcement. With clear guidelines, penalties, and rewards can be properly implemented for those who violate or comply with the regulations. For example, food donation and food bank laws in China should include specific donation processes and tax incentives to encourage participation. Governments should collaborate with non-profits to build a comprehensive food donation platform and provide guidance

---

[6] Liang et al., "Utilizing Landfill Gas."

[7] Brigagão et al., "Zero-Emission Sustainable Landfill-Gas-to-Wire Oxyfuel Process."

for establishing food banks. Article 23 of the Anti-Food Waste Law in China introduces the concept of food donation, but it lacks detailed regulations to support its implementation. Therefore, it is recommended that food donation-related legislation be introduced to specify the donation process, exemption measures, tax incentives, and to encourage enterprises and individuals to donate food.

(3) Target weak areas in plastic and food waste management laws for effective improvements. A full life cycle analysis of food waste management reveals that food donation and recovery laws are the weak links. In China, although anti-food waste laws elevate food waste to a national strategic level, they mainly target consumer-level waste and lack provisions for other stages of the food supply chain. For instance, labeling laws and shelf-life standards for food are not specified, leading to unnecessary food waste. Policymakers should extend anti-food waste regulations to cover the entire food supply chain, optimize labeling laws to avoid unnecessary food loss, and promote the donation of expiring food to food banks. Similarly, for plastic pollution prevention, laws should target small businesses at the end of the supply chain, such as non-chain retail stores and rural bazaars, which are often overlooked. To enhance plastic recycling, regulations should extend to the construction sector and durable goods, ensuring that more types of plastics are collected and recycled.

(4) Update the legal framework to address new kinds of waste and pollutants. Emerging pollutants, such as microplastics, microfibers, and plastic personal protective equipment related to COVID-19, should be incorporated into the legal framework through amendments and new regulations. These new pollutants have not been adequately addressed in current laws and need to be formally recognized to ensure effective management.

(5) Enhance public education on preventing plastic and food waste. Both the US and China should increase efforts to educate the public on the importance of preventing food and plastic waste. This includes promoting a culture of green consumption and low-waste living at the household, community, and societal levels. Campaigns like China's "Clean Plate Campaign" are effective examples that should be expanded to include plastic waste reduction. Similarly, in line with the U.S. Plastics Pact's Roadmap 2.0, we recommend setting ambitious targets such as recycling 50% of plastic packaging by 2030. Additionally, emphasize reuse innovations like returnable cup systems at events to significantly reduce single-use plastics. Promote design for circularity, ensuring all plastic packaging is reusable, recyclable, or compostable by 2030. For instance, Seattle is fostering an integrated reuse system by recruiting partners, making connections, offering incentives, establishing standards for reusable containers, and coordinating systems to ensure reusable items can be used, collected, washed, and redistributed.

Additionally, reducing food waste requires community-wide participation, and information campaigns are crucial for raising awareness and encouraging responsible behavior. Governments, NGOs, schools, suppliers, and other stakeholders should collaborate to promote waste reduction. NGOs can facilitate this by connecting academic experts and practitioners in climate change and waste management with campaign networks to organize conferences and meetings. These events can create social awareness, teach about overlooked waste issues like microplastic pollution, and provide practical skills for responsible action, such as home composting techniques. Incentivizing these campaigns with rewards can enhance their effectiveness, and organizing them as enjoyable activities for families can increase participation and success in educating the public on waste reduction and recycling.

4.3.2 Strengthen the Systematic Collaborative Network and Systems

(1) Create a robust collaborative network to monitor and assess the present municipal waste operation system for improving efficiency. The current municipal waste management network relies on contracts between government bodies and waste management firms for waste collection, transportation, and classification. The efficiency of this system largely depends on the contract system where the government coordinates, bids, and selects reliable and cost-efficient service suppliers. To support supplier selection, a more reliable assessment system is needed, involving social partners such as households, community volunteers, and NGOs. By participating in the assessment system through rewards and credit calculation, these partners can help make municipal waste management more efficient.

While multi-stream approaches to recycling aren't always necessary, implementing advanced mechanical recycling technologies can reduce contamination and increase the quality of recyclables, ultimately boosting recycling rates. The U.S. Plastics Pact's collaborative approach demonstrates the importance of cross-sector partnerships and innovation in achieving these goals. Encourage the development and use of tools similar to the PCR Procurement Toolkit and Design for Circularity Playbooks to support these efforts.

(2) Apply a cohesive collaborative network to reform waste management systems. To reform outdated municipal waste management systems, cities should start separating organic solid waste from disposal, requiring laws, enforcement, community communication, and activities. This effort should involve community volunteers, NGOs, schools, and social enterprises. Additionally, cities should transition from single-stream to dual-stream or multi-stream recycling to reduce contamination and increase recycling rates. Implementing these changes requires collaboration among residents, collection and transportation firms, scientists, and policymakers. Economic incentive policies should also be designed to encourage households and firms to reduce food waste and improve recycling rates. For example, policies could include cash returns for recycling plastic bottles or lower bills for recycling and composting services.

(3) Strengthen collaboration at municipal, city, state, and federal levels to jointly promote relevant laws and policies. Departments in charge of recycling, composting, and disposal should work together to improve collection and transportation efficiency. For example, they can use either separate trucks or segregated bins on a combination truck for waste collection. At the state or interstate level, sharing experiences and collectively advancing waste classification systems can help cities that have not yet separated organic food waste from trash. Improving interagency coordination at the federal level, such as among USDA, EPA, and FDA, can reduce redundancies and leverage complementary activities, making government resource use more efficient and effective.

4.3.3 Introduce Cutting-Edge Approaches and Technologies for Recycling Food Wastes and Plastics

(1) Apply composting and anaerobic digestion technology on a large scale to recycle nutrients and energy from food waste. It is necessary and urgent to implement composting and anaerobic digestion (AD) technologies for food waste (FW) processing. Most cities in the US and China lack awareness and capacity to handle FW properly, leading to landfill dumping. This method increases government budget pressures and causes environmental issues like chemical leachate. Composting and AD technologies should be encouraged to close the waste production loop and support a circular economy. Building renewable plants for composting and AD should involve consultancy and research to select suitable sites, sizes, and types of digester infrastructure. Experimental runs should test efficiency and safety before full-scale implementation. AD technology offers economic benefits through renewable energy production and resource recovery but requires adherence to standards like the Renewable Fuel Standard (RFS). Figure 4.2(a) and (b) shows the technique map for dealing with food waste and a technology roadmap of an example of renewable sites for food waste in Milwaukee, California.

(2) Utilize financial instruments to support composting and AD technology development. City governments should lead by establishing large composting or AD renewable sites to meet municipal FW processing needs. Budget provisions, low-interest loans, and partial ownership sales to renewable energy companies can support these projects. Governments should also integrate processed organic waste materials into renewable energy and fertilizer markets. Encouraging small and medium-sized private renewable sites with subsidies and low-interest loans can stimulate technology adoption and benefit renewable technology development. Experiments with local renewable energy and fuel exchange markets can enhance the economic viability of AD plants and public confidence in sustainable practices. Life cycle assessment (LCA) and life cycle cost analysis (LCCA) are crucial for understanding the long-term success and environmental impact of FW management strategies.

(3) Conduct more research to improve AD and composting technology and reduce environmental impact. Research should focus on improving AD and composting technology to enhance efficiency and reduce environmental impact. Alternative AD processes, such as dark fermentation and arrested methanogenesis,

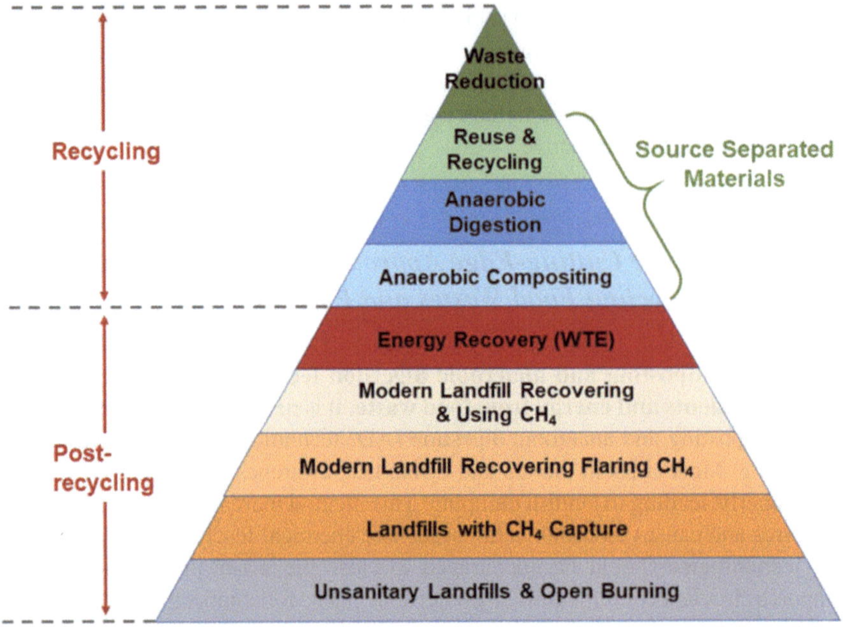

Fig. 4.2 Recycling and post-recycling technologies for managing wastes (Adapted from Tominac et al., 2021) (*Source* Tominac et al. [2021]. *Notes* The figure illustrates system boundaries including transport, processing, and product end use. The system begins with food waste input and tracks waste through transportation and processing via landfill (LFILL), compost (COMP), dry AD (DAD), and wet AD with solid–liquid separation (WAD-SLS) technologies. The transportation network includes the city transport stations. The infrastructure modeled reflects the operating characteristics of the sites in Milwaukee. The environmental impacts and benefits are quantified for each technology. The benefits include the additional products of renewable electricity (i.e., scenarios with AD) and nutrients for crop production when land is applied. It is assumed that these nutrients replace the production and consumption of synthetic fertilizers based on the crop production needs as modeled. Nutrient availability for applied TAN, organic N, P, and K are 100% (after volatilization), and 80% respectively. Grid electricity GHG emissions are specific to WI, and embedded impacts in the production of electricity)

are being developed for biohydrogen and carboxylic acid production. New technologies should be tested to balance environmental impact and renewable energy generation. Large-scale digester operations are viable for urban areas, but cost-effective technologies are needed for smaller scales. Research should aim to increase biogas productivity and yield and reduce biogas upgrading costs. Decentralized AD and composting technologies can offer sustainable solutions for rural and small urban communities. Household composting devices should also be encouraged to create zero FW communities.

(4) Strengthen technology and innovation for plastic degradation. Policymakers should support research on biologically safe methods to degrade plastics, utilizing microorganisms that produce plastic-degrading enzymes. Despite progress, biodegradation and enzymatic degradation of plastics are still in the early stages.

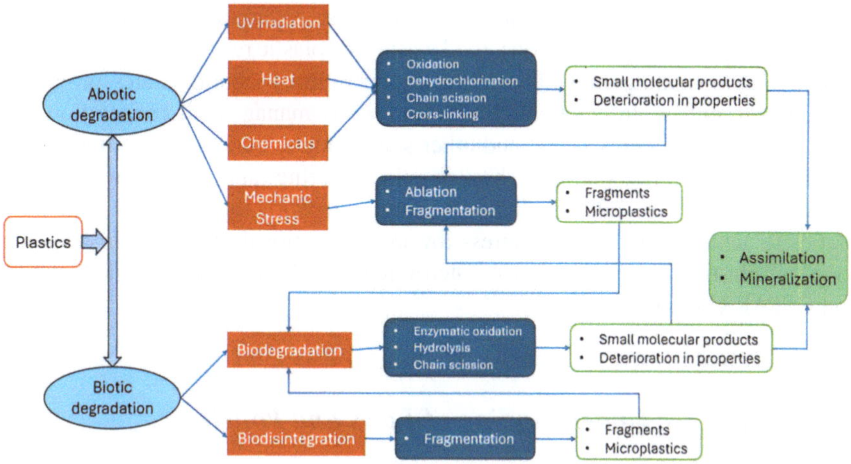

Fig. 4.3 Degradation of plastics schematic diagram (*Source* Zhang et al., 2021)

Research funding should be increased to explore and improve these mechanisms. If feasible, small-scale commercialization should be encouraged by coordinating with investors and large plastic producers. Figure 4.3 shows the current technologies for degrading plastics.

4.4 Integrating waste into US-China climate cooperation priorities

4.4.1 Strengthen Bilateral Dialogue on Waste Management

The U.S. and China should negotiate a specific bilateral agreement focused on waste management, separate from other economic sectors. This agreement should aim to de-securitize the debate over waste management and emphasize shared environmental goals and mutual benefits. Key provisions should include enforcement mechanisms, penalties, and dispute resolution processes. Additionally, the agreement could facilitate the transfer of non-sensitive waste management technologies and joint research initiatives, enabling cost-sharing and more ambitious green technology development.[8]

The purpose of this agreement is to create a structured framework for cooperation in waste management, making cooperation more attractive by ensuring significant mutual benefits, such as technological advancements through joint research. Penalties for non-compliance would make defection costly.

[8] Bains et al., "Trashing the Climate."

Furthermore, the U.S. and China should increase governmental and civil events on climate change, GHG emissions, food waste, and plastic recycling. Both countries should support existing subnational climate cooperation, encourage states, provinces, and cities to engage in practical climate and waste management cooperation, and involve enterprises, think tanks, and other stakeholders. Policymakers should meet periodically for policy dialogue, best practices sharing, and cooperative program facilitation. Internationally, both countries should work together and with other parties to achieve substantial progress toward international objectives in emission, food, and plastics waste management, such as the Paris Agreement, Global Stocktake, and OSPAR Convention.

4.4.2 Increase Understanding of Laws and Policies

Both countries should enhance mutual trust and understanding of each other's legal systems, policy-making processes, legislative enforcement, administrative methods, government ownership boundaries, and project development instruments. Research on related topics, such as fiscal budgets, government decision-making, and household characteristics, should be encouraged to compare waste management in China and the U.S.

Implement policies that support the transition to a circular economy for plastics, where materials are kept within the economy instead of becoming waste. This aligns with the U.S. Plastics Pact's focus on reuse, recycling, and composting. Encourage Extended Producer Responsibility (EPR) to ensure that only essential plastics are produced and used sustainably. Address the social impacts and disparities related to plastic production and use, as highlighted in the Pact's plan. Promote data-driven approaches and industry collaboration to achieve these ambitious goals.

For instance, Seattle strongly encourages the Senate to extend the Solid Waste Infrastructure for Recycling (SWIFR) funding as well as other funding mechanisms, such as the Consumer Recycling Education and Outreach grant program, beyond 2026.

Cooperation on research, investment, consultancy, and marketization projects should be approached with patience and respect, considering the differences in legal and administrative frameworks. It is crucial to account for these differences when developing bilateral legally binding instruments, to facilitate exchanges on mutually agreed topics and enhance pragmatic cooperation.

4.4.3 Emphasize the Data Collaboration

To enhance collaboration on data collection, management, and transparency in waste management between the U.S. and China, both countries should implement integrated systems and adopt advanced technologies. Key steps include:

- **Developing a Comprehensive MRV System**: Establishing an inventory-monitoring-reporting-verification (MRV) system to standardize data collection methods and enhance transparency in reporting emissions, particularly non-CO_2 GHGs like methane and nitrous oxide.[9]
- **Employing Advanced Digital Technologies**: Utilizing big data, AI, machine learning, and cloud computing to improve waste management and recycling processes, especially solving the wide existing problems of inadequate datasets for MSW management for the both two countries. This includes better tracking and sharing of data on waste generation and recycling inputs, enabling informed policy decisions.

Practical suggestions involve creating joint research projects, integrating multidisciplinary research, and setting up nationwide data collection points. Collaborative efforts between universities, research institutes, local governments, and companies are essential for comprehensive data collection and analysis.

4.4.4 Enhance Financial Cooperation

Governments should play a proactive role in encouraging, funding, subsidizing, and marketing renewable and degradation technologies and projects to address critical environmental issues like landfill methane, and food and plastic waste. Specific actions include:

- **Sharing Financial Incentive Methods**: Both the U.S. and China should share experiences in financial incentive methods, such as subsidies, tax exemptions, low-interest loans, rental-free initiatives, and utilities discounts.
- **Fostering Public–Private Partnerships**: Given that many emerging renewable projects cannot be fully marketized early on, both governments should foster public–private partnerships to sustain projects with efficient operation.
- **Promoting Marketization of Renewable Products**: Efforts should focus on pushing the marketization of renewable products from waste-to-energy projects, such as renewable energy, fuel, and fertilizer. These projects should aim to be market-competitive, creating investment opportunities and promoting more waste-to-energy sites and plants.

The U.S. government's investment in recycled waste sorting factories is a good example of generating revenue through selling sorted recycled products. While promoting renewable industries to solve issues related to landfill methane, food waste, and plastic recycling, it is crucial to ensure that products are market-compatible and adhere to regulations and standards. Both governments should study the side effects on employment and the economy as the renewable sector grows and the traditional energy sector diminishes.

[9] Dai and Wang, "Mitigating Methane Emissions."

Additionally, the U.S. and China can collaborate to mobilize international financing, particularly in developing countries, to share renewable and low-emission technologies and practices. This includes utilizing carbon pricing mechanisms and international funding sources, such as the Multilateral Development Banks, to support the transition to low-carbon economies where technical and financial assistance is needed.

4.4.5 Strengthen Collaborate on Research and Technology

The US and China should increase investment in research and development of new technologies essential for mitigating methane emissions and waste impact. Immediate steps should include:

- **Initiating Technical Working Groups**: Establish cooperation on policy dialogue and technical solution exchanges to develop respective methane reduction actions, waste reduction and recycling processes.
- **Encouraging Scientific Communication**: Facilitate communication among scientists from both countries, establish cooperative laboratories in universities and research institutes, provide sufficient research funding, and organize periodic technology exchange conferences.
- **Bridging Technology and Business**: Governments should connect new technologies with business incubators to help renewable projects grow. Preferential policies for talents and programs in renewable technology should be part of the collaborative dialogue.
- **Supporting Market Entry for Technologies**: Introduce venture investors and product resources to grow projects. Encourage transnational investment, acquisition, and mergers to maximize the market value of renewable technologies.

Developing renewable technologies involves not only scientists and researchers but also entrepreneurs, investors, manufacturers, distributors, dealers, and clients. Thus, a mutually beneficial open market is necessary to boost the development of renewable technology for methane and waste from food and plastics.

4.4.6 Promote Exchange Programs to Enhance Communication

Both governments should establish joint training and exchange programs focused on waste management and environmental science to create a platform for exchanging ideas, sharing information, and facilitating meaningful learning. This casual environment allows for real information exchange, providing more context for decision-making and reducing misperceptions. Key steps include:

- **Organizing Multiple Rounds of Exchange and Training Programs**: These programs offer opportunities for professional socialization, shaping policy inclinations and facilitating the dissemination of specific policy approaches.
- **Mitigating Ideological Differences**: These programs help align norms and values in waste management among Chinese and American policymakers, building political trust and potentially leading to mutual preferential treatment in waste management.

This convergence of policy advice among officials and scientists enhances the possibility of transforming cooperative ideas into actionable policies, thereby improving cooperation in waste management.

References

Environmental Protection Agency. (2022). Coalbed Methane Outreach Program (CMOP). https://www.epa.gov/cmop

Qu, S., Guan, D., Ma, Z., & Yi, X. (2019). A Study on the Optimal Path of Methane Emissions Reductions in a Municipal Solid Waste Landfill Treatment Based on the IPCC-SD Model. *Journal of Cleaner Production, 222*, 252–266.

Tominac, P., Aguirre-Villegas, H., Sanford, J., Larson, R., & Zavala, V. (2021). Evaluating Landfill Diversion Strategies for Municipal Organic Waste Management Using Environmental and Economic Factors. *ACS Sustainable Chemistry & Engineering, 9*(1), 489–498. https://doi.org/10.1021/acssuschemeng.0c07784

Zhang, K., Hamidian, A. H., Tubić, A., Zhang, Y., Fang, J. K., Wu, C., & Lam, P. K. (2021). Understanding Plastic Degradation and Microplastic Formation in the Environment: A Review. *Environmental Pollution, 274*, Article 116554.

Chapter 5
Conclusions

This report provides an in-depth analysis of current waste management practices in both countries, focusing on key areas such as landfill methane emissions, food waste management, and plastic recycling. It reviews existing laws and policies and offers pragmatic recommendations for policymakers. Transnational collaboration between the US and China is crucial to leveraging their combined strengths and addressing respective weaknesses, thereby accelerating more effective waste management solutions.

The cooperation between China and the United States in tackling climate change and environmental concerns has made notable strides over recent decades, encompassing both governmental collaboration and non-official business partnerships. Despite existing geopolitical tensions, both nations have consistently pledged joint action during international climate summits, evidenced by the April 2021 U.S.-China Joint Statement Addressing the Climate Crisis and the November 2021 U.S.-China Joint Glasgow Declaration on Enhancing Climate Action in the 2020s.

Much progress has been achieved in reducing greenhouse gas emissions, yet there remains considerable potential for more profound and frequent cooperative efforts. Priorities for advancement include mitigating methane emissions from municipal landfills, promoting plastic recycling, and managing food waste effectively. As significant contributors to food and plastic waste, China and the United States must implement robust waste management policies and enhance recycling practices.

Cooperation should extend beyond high-level dialogues to incorporate diverse forms of interaction and partnership. This includes scientific collaboration, technological innovation, and the joint establishment of climate crisis funds and comprehensive risk management frameworks. Such multi-faceted approaches will strengthen the collaborative efforts laid out in the joint climate declarations.

To foster enhanced cooperation, it is vital to understand and respect differences in historical development, geographical context, population demographics, urbanization levels, and administrative frameworks. While critical thought is necessary, the

H. Huang et al., *Waste Management for Global Sustainability*, CSR, Sustainability, Ethics & Governance, https://doi.org/10.1007/978-981-96-8305-5_5

emphasis should be on pragmatic, actionable progress in key areas of waste management and emission reduction. By pursuing these recommendations, the US and China can lead global efforts in addressing climate change and environmental sustainability, setting a benchmark for international cooperation and achieving substantial environmental benefits.

References

Addo, I. B., Adei, D., & Acheampong, E. O. (2015). Solid Waste Management and Its Health Implications on the Dwellers of Kumasi Metropolis, Ghana. *Current Research Journal of Social Sciences, 7*(2), 81–93.

Bains, P., Brodzinsky, S., Lewis, H., Kelderman, K., & Kelly, L. (2023). Trashing the Climate: Methane from Municipal Landfills.

Balogun, A. L., Adebisi, N., Abubakar, I. R., Dano, U. L., & Tella, A. (2022). Digitalization for Transformative Urbanization, Climate Change Adaptation, and Sustainable Farming in Africa: Trend, Opportunities, and Challenges. *Journal of Integrative Environmental Sciences, 19*(1), 17–37. https://doi.org/10.1080/1943815X.2022.2033791

Blanco, C., Spanbauer, C., & Stienecker, S. (2023, May). America's Broken Recycling System. *California Management Review Insights.* https://cmr.berkeley.edu/2023/05/america-s-broken-recycling-system/

Brad, S. (2024). The Environmental and Health Impacts of Single-Use Plastics and What We Can Do To Reduce Their Use. *The Anella Group.* Accessed March 16, 2024. https://www.vanellagroupmn.com/the-environmental-and-health-impacts-of-single-use-plastics-and-what-we-can-do-to-reduce-their-use

Brigagão, G. V., de Medeiros, J. L., Ofélia de Queiroz, F. A., Mikulčić, H., & Duić, N. (2021). A Zero-Emission Sustainable Landfill-Gas-to-Wire Oxyfuel Process: Bioenergy with Carbon Capture and Sequestration. *Renewable and Sustainable Energy Reviews, 138*, 110686. https://doi.org/10.1016/j.rser.2020.110686

Brolis, L. B., & Platt, B. (2019). *Community Composting Done Right: A Guide to Best Management Practices.* Institute for Local Self-Reliance. https://ilsr.org

Chai, X., Tonjes, D. J., & Mahajan, D. (2016). Methane Emissions as Energy Reservoir: Context, Scope, Causes, and Mitigation Strategies. *Progress in Energy and Combustion Science, 56*, 33–70.

Chandler, A. (2016, July 15). Why Americans Lead the World in Food Waste. *Atlantic.* https://www.theatlantic.com/business/archive/2016/07/american-food-waste/491513/

Charles, D., & Kimman, L. (2021). Plastic Waste Makers Index 2021.

Chenghui, L. With 4% of the World's Population, the United States Produces 17% of the World's Plastic Waste. *Observer.* Accessed April 1, 2024. https://www.guancha.cn/internation/2020_11_03_570136.shtml

China Integrated Waste Management. Evaluation of Kitchen Waste Treatment Technology: A Case Study Based on Case Study. Accessed March 20, 2024. https://iwm-nama.caues.cn/zh-hans/

China NCCC. (2018). *The People's Republic of China Second Biennial Update Report on Climate Change.* https://unfccc.int/sites/default/files/resource/China%202BUR_English.pdf

H. Huang et al., *Waste Management for Global Sustainability*, CSR, Sustainability, Ethics & Governance, https://doi.org/10.1007/978-981-96-8305-5

Community Compost Platform LIEE. Building and Sharing a Green Community: Zero-Distance Composting for Jixiang Garden Residents. Accessed April 15, 2024. https://mp.weixin.qq.com/s/MUGZIppcxtW7pg3j1x6Fng

Community Compost Platform LIEE. List of Practice Partners for Community Kitchen Waste Composting Platform 2024. Accessed April 15, 2024. https://mp.weixin.qq.com/s/voQIv7U8yuA4wyezpfGhDw

Cordier, M., Uehara, T., Baztan, J., et al. (2021). Plastic Pollution and Economic Growth: The Influence of Corruption and Lack of Education. *Ecological Economics, 182*, Article 106930. https://doi.org/10.1016/j.ecolecon.2020.106930

Dai, F., & Wang, Y. (2024). Mitigating Methane Emissions: Domestic and Joint Efforts by the United States and China. *Environmental Science and Ecotechnology, 20.*

Ding, Y., Zhao, J., Liu, J.-W., Zhou, J., Cheng, L., Zhao, J., Shao, Z., Iris, Ç., Pan, B., Li, X., & Hu, Z.-T. (2021). A Review of China's Municipal Solid Waste (MSW) and Comparison with International Regions: Management and Technologies in Treatment and Resource Utilization. *Journal of Cleaner Production, 293*, Article 126144.

Environmental Protection Agency. (2021). Advancements in U.S. Recycling and Waste Management. https://www.epa.gov/

Environmental Protection Agency. Food: Material-Specific Data. Last modified October 5, 2023. Accessed March 25, 2024. https://www.epa.gov/facts-and-figures-about-materials-waste-and-recycling/food-material-specific-data

Environmental Protection Agency. Quantifying Methane Emissions from Landfilled Food Waste. Last modified January 22, 2024. Accessed March 25, 2024. https://www.epa.gov/land-research/quantifying-methane-emissions-landfilled-food-waste

Environmental Protection Agency. (2018). *Advancing Sustainable Materials Management: 2018 Fact Sheet.*

Evans, A. I., & Nagele, R. M. (2018). A Lot to Digest: Advancing Food Waste Policy in the United States. *Natural Resources Journal, 58*(1), 177–214.

Executive Office of the President. (2023, April 26). Executive Order 14096: Revitalizing Our Nation's Commitment to Environmental Justice for All. *Federal Register*. https://www.federalregister.gov/documents/2023/04/26/2023-08955/revitalizing-our-nations-commitment-to-environmental-justice-for-all

Executive Office of the President. (2021, December 13). Executive Order No. 14057: Catalyzing Clean Energy Industries and Jobs Through Federal Sustainability. *Federal Register*. https://www.federalregister.gov/documents/2021/12/13/2021-27114/catalyzing-clean-energy-industries-and-jobs-through-federal-sustainability

Gangira, L. How Does Food Waste Affect the Environment? *Earth.org*. Accessed March 14, 2024. https://earth.org/how-does-food-waste-affect-the-environment/

Garbage Sorting and Recycling in the United States: The Rules Are Fine and the Management Is Weak. (2019). *Economic Reference Network*. Accessed March 20, 2024. https://finance.sina.cn/2019-08-06/detail-ihytcerm8747979.d.html?from=wap

Gines, K. B. (2019). Food Waste: Regulatory Game? *Drake Journal of Agricultural Law, 24*(1), 97–116.

Greenpeace. A Low-Carbon Code for Kitchen Waste. Accessed February 27, 2024. https://www.greenpeace.org.cn/food-waste/

Guangping, G. (2023). Global Efforts to Control Marine Plastic Waste. *Ecological Economy, 39*(04), 1–4.

Haines, G. (2021, March 16). The Holy Grail of Aviation: Net-Zero Flights 'On the Horizon', Say Scientists. *Positive News*. Accessed March 25, 2024. https://www.positive.news/science/net-zero-flights-on-the-horizon-say-scientists/

Hardesty, B., Wilcox, C., Lawson, T., Lansdell, M., & van der Velde, T. (2014). Understanding the Effects of Marine Debris on Wildlife: Report to Earthwatch Australia. Commonwealth Scientific and Industrial Research Organization (CSIRO).

He, P., Chen, L., Shao, L., Zhang, H., & Lü, F. (2019). Municipal Solid Waste (MSW) Landfill: A Source of Microplastics? Evidence of Microplastics in Landfill Leachate. *Water Research, 159*, 38–45.

Huang, X., & Rao, N. (2021). Overseas Investigation and Reference of Food Saving Legislation. *Journal of Chongqing University (Social Science Edition)*, 101.

Institute for Local Self-Reliance. Composting for Community Map. Accessed 2024. https://ilsr.org/composting/map/

IPCC. (2019). *2019 Refinement to the 2006 IPCC Guidelines for National Greenhouse Gas Inventories.*

IPCC. (2023). *Climate Change 2023 Synthesis Report.*

Jiacheng, L. (2023). The Fourth Anniversary of Garbage Classification: The Reduction Is Successful, and the Incineration Situation Is Embarrassing. *China Dialogue.*

Kirsten, J., et al. From Farm to Kitchen: The Environmental Impacts of U.S. Food Waste. U.S. Environmental Protection Agency Office of Research and Development. Accessed March 21, 2024. https://www.epa.gov/land-research/farm-kitchen-environmental-impacts-us-food-waste

Kish, R. (2018). Using Legislation to Reduce One-Time Plastic Bag Usage. *Economic Affairs, 38*(2), 224–239. https://doi.org/10.1111/ecaf.12287

Landfill Methane Outreach Program (LMOP). (2015). *LFG Energy Project Development Handbook.* Paged in sections. https://www3.epa.gov/lmop/documents/pdfs/pdf_full.pdf

Landwall, C. Single-Use Plastics 101. *NRDC.* Accessed March 15, 2024. https://www.nrdc.org/stories/single-use-plastics-101#ban

Larsen, J., & Venkova, S. (2014). Plan B Updates—The Downfall of the Plastic Bag: A Global Picture. *Earth Policy Institute.* https://www.earth-policy.org/plan_b_updates/2014/update123

Li, J. (2023, September 4). Four Years of Waste Sorting Leaves China's Incinerators Short of Fuel. *China Dialogue.* https://chinadialogue.net/en/cities/four-years-of-waste-sorting-leaves-chinas-incinerators-short-of-fuel/

Liang, X., Goh, H. H., Kurniawan, T. A., Zhang, D., Dai, W., Liu, H. et al. (2022). Utilizing Landfill Gas (LFG) to Electrify Digital Data Centers in China for Accelerating Energy Transition in Industry 4.0 Era. *Journal of Cleaner Production, 369*, 133297.

Lin, J., Dai, F., Zheng Khanna, N. et al. (2022). Reducing Methane Emissions in the U.S. and China.

Linlin, L., et al. (2023). Recycling Status of Post-Consumer Plastics in the Context of 'Dual Carbon' and Its Application in Food. *The Plastics Industry, 51*(08), 1–8+24.

Ma, S., Zhou, C., Chi, C., Liu, Y., & Yang, G. (2020). Estimating Physical Composition of Municipal Solid Waste in China by Applying Artificial Neural Network Method. *Environmental Science & Technology, 54*(15), 9609–9617.

Margaret Popoola, B. (2023). Biodegradable Waste. In *IntechOpen.* https://doi.org/10.5772/intechopen.107910

Meiffren-Swango, C., Engstrom, J., & Sokolow, L. (2024, January 17). Plastic Bag Bans Work. *Environment America.* https://environmentamerica.org/center/resources/plastic-bag-bans-work/

Michael, N., et al. (2017). Study on the Recovery and Utilization of Biomass Components from Municipal Solid Waste in China. Federal Ministry for the Environment, Nature Conservation, Building and Nuclear Safety.

National Bureau of Statistics. (2023). *China Statistical Yearbook 2023.* China Statistics Press. https://www.stats.gov.cn/sj/ndsj/2023/indexch.htm

National Conference of State Legislators. (2020). State Plastic and Paper Bag Legislations. National Conference of State Legislators (NCSL). https://www.ncsl.org/research/environment-and-natural-resources/plastic-bag-legislation.aspx

National Development and Reform Commission, Ministry of Housing and Urban-Rural Development. (2016, December). 13th Five-Year Plan for the Development of Urban Living Waste Sorting and Treatment Facilities. Accessed March 25, 2024. https://www.ndrc.gov.cn/resource/W020190905497906455466.pdf

National Development and Reform Commission, Ministry of Housing and Urban-Rural Development. (2021, May). 14th Five-Year Plan for the Development of Urban Living Waste Sorting and

Treatment Facilities. Accessed March 25, 2024. http://big5.www.gov.cn/gate/big5/www.gov.cn/zhengce/zhengceku/2021-05/14/5606349/files/bd8ca92c767f4b8786b9374a76e0d1fd.pdf

National Overview: Facts and Figures on Materials, Wastes and Recycling. (2023). *EPA.gov*. Accessed November 22, 2023. https://www.epa.gov/facts-and-figures-about-materials-waste-and-recycling/national-overview-facts-and-figures-materials

Nielsen, T., Holmberg, K., & Stripple, J. (2019). Need a Bag? A Review of Public Policies on Plastic Carrier Bags—Where, How and to What Effect? *Waste Management, 87*, 429–440. https://doi.org/10.1016/j.wasman.2019.02.025

Nirappil, F. (2014, September 30). California Becomes First State to Ban Plastic Bags. *Associated Press News*. https://apnews.com

Office for Science, London. (2021). Update of the 2010 Retail Bags Report. T.G. Townsend, M. Anshassi, N.M. Robey, N. Steffen, F. Gonzales, A. Ricketts, J. Bielecki.

Owojori, O., Edokpayi, J. N., Mulaudzi, R. & Odiyo, J. O. (2020). Characterisation, Recovery and Recycling Potential of Solid Waste in a University of a Developing Economy. https://doi.org/10.3390/su12125111

Penman, J., Kruger, D., Galbally, I., Hiraishi, T., Nyenzi, B., Emmanuel, S., Buendia, L., Hoppaus, R., Martinsen, T., Meijer, J., Miwa, K., & Tanabe, K. (Eds.). (2000). *Good Practice Guidance and Uncertainty Management in National Greenhouse Gas Inventories*. Institute for Global Environmental Strategies. https://www.ipcc.ch/publication/good-practice-guidance-and-uncertainty-management-in-national-greenhouse-gas-inventories/

Pollution Act | Break Free From Plastic. Accessed June 3, 2024. https://www.breakfreefromplastic.org/pollution-act/

Poore, J., & Nemecek, T. (2018). Reducing Food's Environmental Impacts Through Producers and Consumers. *Science, 360*(6392), 987–992.

Powell, J. T., Townsend, T. G., & Zimmerman, J. B. (2015). Estimates of Solid Waste Disposal Rates and Reduction Targets for Landfill Gas Emissions. *Nature Climate Change*. https://doi.org/10.1038/NCLIMATE2804

Preeti. The Impact of Single-Use Plastics on the Environment. *Scale Climate Action*. Accessed March 15, 2024. https://scaleclimateaction.org/environment/the-impact-of-single-use-plastics-on-the-environment/

Priefer, C., Jörissen, J., & Bräutigam, K.-R. (2016). Food Waste Prevention in Europe—A Cause-Driven Approach to Identify the Most Relevant Leverage Points for Action. *Resources, Conservation and Recycling, 109*, 155–165. https://doi.org/10.1016/j.resconrec.2016.03.004

Prince George's County Government. Organics Composting Facility. Accessed 2024. https://www.princegeorgescountymd.gov/departments-offices/environment/waste-recycling/facilities/organics-composting-facility

Ranniger, G. (2020, June 4). Plastic Pollution Explained. *Environmental Health News*. https://www.ehn.org/plastic-pollution-101-2646027569/plastic-pollution-the-problem

Ren, F. (2019). Collaborative Governance Approaches to Food Safety in Supply Chain Management. *Hebei Law Science*, 140.

Rep. Pallone, F. H.R.1321—114th Congress (2015–2016): Microbead-Free Waters Act of 2015. *Legislation*. December 28, 2015. https://www.congress.gov/bill/114th-congress/house-bill/1321

Romer, J., & Tamminen, L. (2014). Plastic Bag Reduction Ordinances: New York City's Proposed Charge on All Carryout Bags as a Model for U.S. Cities. *Tulane Environmental Law Journal, 27*(2), 237–275.

Romer, J. R. (2010). The Evolution of San Francisco's Plastic Bag Ban. *Golden Gate University Environmental Law Journal, 40*(2)

Saalah, S., et al. (2020). Management of Biodegradable Plastic Waste: A Review. *Advances in Waste Processing Technology*, 127–143.

Sen. Merkley, J. (2023, October 25). Titles—S.3127—118th Congress (2023–2024): Break Free From Plastic Pollution Act of 2023. *Legislation*. https://www.congress.gov/bill/118th-congress/senate-bill/3127/titles

Sen. Portman, R. (2021, March 23). S.923—117th Congress (2021–2022): RECYCLE Act of 2021. *Legislation.* https://www.congress.gov/bill/117th-congress/senate-bill/923

Sen. Sullivan, D. (2020, December 18). Text - S.1982 - 116th Congress (2019–2020): Save Our Seas 2.0 Act. *Legislation.* https://www.congress.gov/bill/116th-congress/senate-bill/1982/text

Shen, G., Li, Z., Hong, T., Ru, X., Wang, K., Gu, Y. et al. (2023). The Status of the Global Food Waste Mitigation Policies: Experience and Inspiration for China. *Environment, Development and Sustainability*, 1–29.

Shen, M., Huang, W., Chen, M., Song, B., Zeng, G., & Zhang, Y. (May 2020). (Micro)Plastic Crisis: Un-Ignorable Contribution to Global Greenhouse Gas Emissions and Climate Change. *Journal of Cleaner Production, 254*, Article 120138. https://doi.org/10.1016/j.jclepro.2020.120138

Shilei, H., & Zong, F. (2023). Treatment Methods and Development Trend of Waste Biodegradable Plastics. *China Environmental Science, 43*(12), 6445–6464.

Sikder, S., Toha, M., & Mostafizur Rahman, M. (2024). An Overview on Municipal Solid Waste Characteristics and Its Impacts on Environment and Human Health. In *Technical Landfills and Waste Management: Volume 1: Landfill Impacts, Characterization and Valorisation*, 135–155. OECD Stat. Extracts. Online database; 2024.

Sineng, Z., et al. (2019). Microplastics in the Environment and Their Effects on Human Health. *China Plastics, 33*(4), 81–88.

Solid Waste Observation Public Account. Development and Environmental Management Status of Domestic Waste Landfill in Foreign Countries. Accessed March 17, 2024. http://www.envirunion.com/newsinfo-34760.html

Sun, C., et al. (2022). Progress in Upcycling Polylactic Acid Waste as an Alternative Carbon Source: A Review. *Progress in Polymer Science, 446*(1), Article 136881.

Sun, J., Zhu, Z. R., Li, W. H., Yan, X. F., Wang, L. K., Zhang, L., Jin, J. B., Dai, X. H., & Ni, B. J. (2021). Revisiting Microplastics in Landfill Leachate: Unnoticed Tiny Microplastics and Their Fate in Treatment Works. *Water Research, 190*, Article 116784.

Suzanne Goldenberg. (2016, July 13). Half of All US Food Produce Is Thrown Away, New Research Suggests. *The Guardian.* https://www.theguardian.com/environment/2016/jul/13/us-food-waste-ugly-fruit-vegetables-perfect?CMP=share_btn_tw

Technology Leader. Plastic in Landfills Never Degrades, Did You Know That? *China Association of Circular Economy.* Accessed March 15, 2024. https://www.chinacace.org/news/view?id=11199

Teuten, E., Saquing, J. M., Knappe, D. R. U., Barlaz, M. A., Jonsson, S., Björn, A., Rowland, S. J., Thompson, R. C., Galloway, T. S., Yamashita, R., Ochi, D., Watanuki, Y., Moore, C., Viet, P. H., Tana, T. S., Prudente, M., Boonyatumanond, R., Zakaria, M. P., Akkhavong, K., & Takada, H. (2009). Transport and Release of Chemicals from Plastics to the Environment and to Wildlife. *Philosophical Transactions of the Royal Society B, 364*, 2027–2045. https://doi.org/10.1098/rstb.2008.0284

Themelis, N. J., & Ma, W. (2021). Waste to Energy (WTE) in China: From Latecomer to Front Runner. *Waste Disposal & Sustainable Energy, 3*, 267–274.

Themelis, N. J., & Ulloa, P. A. (2007). Methane Generation in Landfills. *Renewable Energy, 32*(7), 1243–1257.

Thompson, R. (2017). Future of the Sea: Plastic Pollution. UK Government.

United Nations Environment Programme, and Climate and Clean Air Coalition. Global Methane Assessment: Benefits and Costs of Mitigating Methane Emissions (2021). https://www.unep.org/resources/report/global-methane-assessment-benefits-and-costs-mitigating-methane-emissions

United Nations Environment Programme. Food Waste Index Report 2024. Think Eat Save: Tracking Progress to Halve Global Food Waste. Last modified March 27, 2024. Accessed April 1, 2024. https://wedocs.unep.org/20.500.11822/45230

United States Environmental Protection Agency. (2023). 2019 Wasted Food Report.

United States Government Accountability Office. (2020). Building on Existing Federal Efforts Could Help Address Cross-Cutting Challenges. Report to Congressional Requesters. United States Government Accountability Office. https://www.gao.gov/assets/d2187.pdf

US EPA, O. (2019, November 13). National Recycling Strategy. Reports and Assessments. https://www.epa.gov/circulareconomy/national-recycling-strategy
Wagner, T. (2017). Reducing Single-Use Plastic Shopping Bags in the USA. *Waste Management, 70*, 3–12. https://doi.org/10.1016/j.wasman.2017.09.003
Wan, J., Feng, X., Tang, Q., et al. (2019). Cost-Benefit Analysis of Harmless Disposal of Municipal Solid Waste: A Case Study of 25 Cities in China. *Resources and Industries, 21*(4), 81–89.
Wang, X., Cai, Y., Chaoqun Tan, et al. (2023). Preparation and Performance of Gel-Based Slow-Release Nitrogen Fertilizer from Kitchen Waste Pretreated by Thermally Activated Persulfate. *Journal of Environmental Engineering, 17*(4), 1327–1336.
Wasted Food Scale. (2023). US EPA. Accessed April 16, 2024. https://www.epa.gov/sustainable-management-food/wasted-food-scale
Weber Consulting. (2020). Overview of the Waste Incineration Power Generation Industry in the United States: Includes Development History, Business Model, and Analysis of Leading. *Polaris Waste Power Grid*, 2020. Accessed December 2, 2023. https://mhuanbao.bjx.com.cn/mnews/20201202/1119449.shtml
Weiss, J. I. (2019). Extended Producer Responsibility and the Environmental Policy Implementation Process in California: A Case Study of Paintcare. Master's Thesis, San Jose State University, San Jose, CA, USA. https://doi.org/10.31979/etd.mm8b-bv86
Wen, Z., Zhang, Y., Fu., & Daishi. (2019). Environmental Impact of a Takeaway Order Based on Whole Industry Chain Assessment. *China Environmental Science, 39*(9), 8.
Wenjie, L., & Hua, L. (2021). Overview of Low Carbon Management of Kitchen Waste Throughout Life Cycle. *All-China Environment Federation.*
World Bank. (2018). Solid Waste Management. Accessed January 20, 2024. http://www.worldbank.org/en/topic/urbandevelopment/brief/solid-waste-management
Xanthos, D., & Walker, T. (2017). International Policies to Reduce Plastic Marine Pollution from Single-Use Plastics (Plastic Bags and Microbeads): A Review. *Marine Pollution Bulletin, 118*(1–2), 17–26. https://doi.org/10.1016/j.marpolbul.2017.02.048
Yu, C., Jin, D., Hu, X., He, W., & Li. G. (2023). An Overview of Management Status and Recycling Strategies for Plastic Packaging Waste in China. *Recycling.*
Yu, S., Behrendt, J., Zhu, M., Cheng, X., Li, W., Liu, B. et al. (2022). Roadmap for US-China Methane Collaboration: Methane Emissions, Mitigation Potential, and Policies Summary for Policymakers.
Zhang, H., Liu, G., Xue, L., Zuo, J., Chen, T., Vuppaladadiyam, A., & Duan, H. (2020). Anaerobic Digestion-Based Waste-to-Energy Technologies Can Halve the Climate Impact of China's Fast-Growing Food Waste by 2040. *Journal of Cleaner Production, 277*, Article 123490.
Zhang, Y., & Wen, Z. (2022). Mapping the Environmental Impacts and Policy Effectiveness of the Takeaway Food Industry in China. *Science of the Total Environment, 808*, Article 152023.
Zhou, J., Zheng, C., Zhang, C., et al. (2022). Research on the Current Situation of Kitchen Waste as Feed. *Guangdong Chemical Industry, 49*(24), 193–195.

MIX
Papier aus verantwortungsvollen Quellen
Paper from responsible sources
FSC® C105338

If you have any concerns about our products,
you can contact us on
ProductSafety@springernature.com

In case Publisher is established outside the EU,
the EU authorized representative is:
Springer Nature Customer Service Center GmbH
Europaplatz 3, 69115 Heidelberg, Germany

Printed by Libri Plureos GmbH
in Hamburg, Germany